MY BLEEDING BUSINESS

TERRY DOWNES

My Bleeding Business

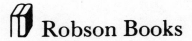 Robson Books

Original hardback edition published in 1964

This updated paperback edition first published in Great Britain in 1989 by Robson Books Ltd, Bolsover House, 5–6 Clipstone Street, London W1P 7EB.

British Library Cataloguing in Publication Data

Downes, Terry
  My bleeding business.
  1. Boxing.   Downes, Terry
  I. Title
  796.8'3'0924

ISBN 0 86051 373 4

Printed in Great Britain by
Billing & Sons Ltd., Worcester

To

My dad who taught me left from
right and right from wrong.

And to my four kids, Wendy, Terry,
Paul and Richard, to show 'em what a
good old man they've got.

The Reason Why

In Glasgow, former world middle-weight champion Terry Downes punches his way through 10 rounds to defeat the American light-heavy-weight, Ed Zaremba.

Some people may wonder why he bothered to do it at all. For Terry Downes has a stake in a £500,000 betting-shop empire. He is a rich man, and has no need to fight.

The truth is that he likes boxing. He enjoys it as much as the sports-lovers who gain such pleasure from seeing him in the ring.

That is why he is so good at it.

Daily Express 1964

Contents

Illustrations

Introduction
IN MY CORNER

I always wanted to publish a book about my life, fights, and thoughts, and the people I meet. But I haven't got the patience to write more than two postcards. I needed somebody to put my words on paper.

I asked REG GUTTERIDGE to record my words and thoughts so that you might even understand them. Apart from being a knowledgeable and respected boxing journalist and commentator, Reg comes from a fighting family. He reported nearly all my fights, criticized or praised me from ringsides in Britain and America.

I stress that Reg did not always agree with my views, but respected my right to record them. I don't always agree with him. When I won the world and British middle-weight championships he tipped the other guy. We all make mistakes!

But without his help this book, both the first edition and this new updated version, would not have been possible—for better or worse. I want to say 'Thanks' to him. Well done, me son.

One of the Downes Kids

I MUST have been a bit of a big-head from the off. I weighed in at 8½ lb. in Paddington Hospital, London, on May 9, 1936. Anyway, my mum, who was there at the time, says I was black-and-blue the moment I came into the world—with fists clenched!—so I suppose you can say I was conditioned for the ole bruises the moment the doctor slapped my rump to begin the breathing.

If I cried at the time I've got to admit it was the only time I've ever objected to pats on the back. Now I love 'em. And I don't cry about being black-and-blue now and then. Nobody bleeds for glory; you do it to get a nice few quid, make something of yourself, become a somebody.

I ain't a hypocrite. I've loved every minute of it. Well, most of it. Getting whacked is not exactly my idea of enjoyment, but unless you've boxed a bit it's hard to explain the satisfaction you can get from a decent punch-up. I've been a bit of a lad at times, got into a few scraps as a kid, but I don't consider myself a violent geezer. I don't think I use boxing to unload any in-born streaks of meanness, or channel the violence, like them psychiatrists say. Besides, anyone who goes to a psychiatrist needs his head examined.

Me, I'm a fighter because it's something I do pretty good. If I hadn't been good enough to be a pro and battle for a few quid I'd still have been fighting amateur now. Only when the old battery inside me runs down will I quit. Keeping the body in shape has helped keep the mind working, too.

Anyway, that weigh-in must have been a bit hectic. I must have given mum a bad time—though, blimey, she's still a cracker in my book—because she scrubbed out the idea of having more kids. In those days most of the Cockney families were big mobs. Having kids was all the rage. Could be that sex-talk wasn't so open them days and the married people just weren't 'with it'. Anyway, there were so many Downes kids around Paddington I swear the family used to call 'em all in and share 'em out at Christmas. My dad—I used to call him the Old Man, but I'm going all posh in this book—took an oath the Downeses are the biggest family in England—and wants to stick his money up for a bet. It gets a tough job trying to remember all the names.

My dad was just one of *sixteen* brothers—his mum was a real champ!—so it was only natural for me to expect being lumbered with a few more brothers or sisters. The form book pointed to it. Anyway, Mum retired after having me (how right she was!) and we've been a happy little foursome ever since. I have every right to be proud of my mum and dad, and sister Sylvie, too. (Her real name is Sylvia.)

The Downeses of Paddington were a right notorious mob. If you've seen Paddington you can understand how the surroundings produce a tough breed. It's a bit of an asphalt jungle. It's known mainly because of the station that brings all that country mob from the West into the Smoke. When I was a kid I used to climb the railway wall and watch the Great West service rattling along, mainly from Wales.

If you're on the train you look out at all those windows—most of them need a scrub—and wonder what kind of rat-trap that must be to live in. The washing waves in the backyards with engine smoke choking the little basement kitchens. Those grim tenements give the fresh-air visitors the creeps. But you're happy—sometimes—being raised with all that action around you. It all helps to make you alert. Cockneys give the needle to a lot of provincials, or foreigners, because they chat quick and can spot a chance to make a few bob.

It's all part of hustling to survive in a big city, where it takes longer to make friends and where people don't care two hoots what the neighbours do. But the Londoner is second to none when it comes to digging his hand in his pocket, bunging a few quid about, or being a real mate. They're great stickers, the Cockneys. Real warm-hearted people. I'm not saying they're better than anyone else, but they ain't any worse.

And a shrewd Dr. Sam Johnson, the educated old boy, who had a few more readers than me, wrote: 'When a man is tired of London he is tired of life.' See what I mean?

We Downeses, as I said, typified the Paddington Cockney, though you'd have to have a smashing pair of ears to hear the sound of Bow Bells from London, W.2.

We weren't murderers or mobsters, but I can't pretend we were always a bunch of do-gooders. One or two of the uncles, I'm sure, did a bit of villainy in their day. Nothing terrible, like, but not exactly the sort of moves the Law thought was funny.

I now know there was nothing clever in that. But those days were hard in the grubby London back streets. You couldn't cadge a nice few bob off the National Assistance like you can today. I've always thought that's a right show-up the way we stand for people coming into this country and copping money. I'm all for the principle of National Assistance, especially when I see those old 'uns struggling to afford a crust and a bit of comfort.

But I get the dead needle hearing tales about layabouts spinning a yarn and getting a few quid regularly. I've heard of geezers with big families who find it less profitable to work than cop on the National Assistance. But that's for the politicians to sort out. From what I can see of it they could do with one or two more useful punchers in Parliament.

When I was brought up the work just wasn't around for many to better themselves. You had to be a bit of a grafter to keep grub on the table. And my dad made sure we never went short of a crust or clothes on our back. I ate like a horse—and still do.

When he first got married Dad was a regular soldier—that was the best way he knew of getting a living without working!— and anyone less likely to stand for discipline was Dick Downes. But, so he reckons, he wasn't a bad soldier at the time. He'd also done a fair stint with the Red Cross (came in handy when

I started shedding a few splashes of blood). It wasn't until he started chasing Hilda Harwood that he began going off the rails, like forgetting to go back from leave on time. He'd found a good partner. It's turned out a smashing match, with, of course, the usual ups and downs.

Dick Downes was too smart an old soldier to step on the toes of the Law, and in case you're expecting me to start blowing it about that I've done some bird—that's prison—you're gonna be disappointed.

I've had a look at some of those clever geezers who've had their fair share of prison porridge and they don't look too healthy to me. I mean telling the kids you've been working away, or on holiday, ain't no game. They don't look all that brown. One minute they've got plenty, then they've got nothing and had to pay for it. There just ain't no future in that.

They invite me often to go and chat with the boys in the Nick. It gets a bit embarrassing when one of the cons yells out, 'How's your cousin so-and-so getting on?', but watching them with that prison-grey look and uniform makes me realize even more it can't be smart being there.

I'm not saying I ain't bent a rule now and then, done silly things, but never come to any harm. Dad always says I walk away from trouble and I'm not saying he's wrong. Besides, if I'd stepped out of line the ole man—sorry Dad—would have given me a right tanning. So he and Mum deserve some credit. I often think a good whack now and then can straighten out a little terror quicker than a chat.

I liked winning too much even as a kid that when I could see the Law never came second I knew it was stupid trying to beat it. I hope I'm game enough in the ring, but outside I'm a bit of a charley when it comes to busting the Law. There just ain't any sense in it. The most that's happened to me is a parking ticket, a few choice words with the copper who thinks he's booked a murderer instead of a motorist, a bit of 'can' in the U.S. Marines, an occasional friendly chat with the guv'nor of my local Law, and the official prison talks.

As for getting money easy, being around with Dad cured me of that. He's been a good fiddler all his life. He'd buy a car sell it, buy another one. He'd earn a pound or two here and there, without ever standing for office hours, to keep us going. But he used to have a right bug for them dogs—greyhound racing, I mean. I'm not kidding, he used to spend his holidays on the dog tracks. There used to be right murders among us because of it.

Dad would, maybe, fancy a last-minute bet on the Tote after he'd weighed up the dogs parading. He'd look at them like dogs were going out of circulation, almost counting the hairs on their tails. He reckoned he knew a fast or fit dog by its condition. As the dogs were being pushed into the six traps he'd insist on a bet, and Mum, or me, would scarper off to a Tote betting window. What was the use of coming back after his dog had won and trying to explain that the Tote was closed before we got on?

Like I said, there used to be murders. So I'd seen enough, as a kid, to forget any ideas about getting money easy. Now I can go now and then to watch dog-racing in comfort, even owned a fair old greyhound, presented a few prizes, and found the modern set-up far more respectable.

Mind you, fighting ain't exactly the easiest way of getting rich—but at least it's honest. It's hard graft. But more boys go out with than without money.

I suppose I started learning, or trying to learn, about life being sent to a nursery school down the Harrow Road. They called it the Tin School because it had a corrugated-iron roof. All I really remember about it was being given beds to have a kip every afternoon. I had nothing against that. But before I could get accustomed to laying about that mug Hitler started his battle and the next thing I know they're putting cardboard name-tags around my neck and bunging me off to the country.

Stand on me, anyone who stayed the course during the war living in blacked-out London got a right bashing from bombs, buzz-bombs, rockets, and Gawd knows what else. They were marvellous to stand it. But, naturally, most mothers fancied getting their kids out of the way. With kids of my own I can now appreciate that feeling even more. A big thing about the Cockney families is their feeling for kids.

B

People who have suffered through a war don't go around doing things for kicks. They just seek peace. When you've had a bomb or two dropping on a home, and seen them pulling kids out of debris, it stops all talk about future wars. That's a game where nobody wins. My granny ran a boarding house in Paddington. I think we lived with her for a while, and when she rounded up all the Downes kids some of them looked like they'd been dug up from under the floorboards. Talk about Fagin's kitchen! Her place was a sort of corral. Our family couldn't leave London like anyone else. Oh, no. The Downeses were herded off, mob-handed, to Newbridge, in Cornwall, which ain't too far from Land's End. So you see they did their best to get well rid of us. It was the nearest thing to nowhere they could sort out. One push and we're all in the sea.

I think they might have closed Paddington's Senior Street School when the Downes kids moved out. They bunged us on trains or coaches—we used to call 'em charabancs—and scattered us about this Newbridge. When you're just a kid you think the whole world has gone stone raving mad by whipping you away from home and Mum. I'm with my cousin Pat's little sister in some lonely little house, and my sister Sylvie, who is two years older than me, is with Pat's elder sister. Pat and I never thought then that we'd be partners in big business.

They've broke the family up and that's no game. We're all feeling like we've been belted for doing something wrong, but we just don't understand this lousy war business. Well, we're standing this shock well for a few weeks. I remember I hated the cold custard.

I'm just learning to understand the Cornish accent, and I'm looking in a shop-window with Sylvie, when I spot my mum asking some strangers if they'd seen us.

She'd come all the way down from London—it's some 300-odd miles—to see how we're getting on. She didn't even know where we were living. She just got off a bus and began asking questions. You ought to have seen her face when I called out 'Mum'. I don't think she'd expected us to be out in town on our own. But I wasn't arf glad to see her.

Right away she tumbles we ain't all that happy being broken

up, so, bang, she and my aunt go and chat a local farmer. If
there's one thing the Downeses do well it's chatting. Next
thing we know all the family kids are being rounded up as if
the Germans are about to invade us and we're trailing off
behind Mum and Aunt like the Pied Piper to take over a
farmhouse. There must have been thirty of us. We're all
together again. It's an 'andsome take-over. My first.

Dad did his bit in the war like a million others. Having
copped pay for nearly nothing with the Army in peacetime,
he went into the R.E.M.E. (Royal Electrical and Mechanical
Engineers). He loved engines, and knew about them, so
he must have been handy with the R.E.M.E.—when he wasn't
on the run! Mind you, he did his stint in Africa and Italy and
if I had time and space I'd tell you how he won the war. Well,
that's his story.

I remember down in Cornwall how we used to see Dad or
may be an uncle or elder cousins, come creeping down to see
us in the middle of the night. They were probably dodging
the Military Police or up to some caper. But the kids always
came first. Some of them had hitch-hiked it.

We more or less became accustomed to this evacuation lark,
staying maybe a year down in Cornwall, before the really
big bombing had begun in London. They had nasty bombing
around the docks, and a few strays, but the naughty stuff
was to come. Anyway, blood being thicker than water, Mum
must have decided she'd rather take a chance and have Sylvie
and me home. So back we went.

We lived in Westbourne Terrace and I remember being half
scared out of my life when a bomb fell in Bourne Terrace,
which was only a stone's throw away, and the blast blew Mum
down the stairs. I was only six—but the memory of that scare
is still there.

I went to St. Saviour's School, and because Dad was away
in the Army, Mum had to work and rush home to get us some
grub. Kids during those times grew up fast. You had to fend
for yourself. The dads were all soldiering and mums had to
graft to make ends meet. We were no different. Sylvie became
like a second mother when she was only about nine. She'd

come home from school and get some tea for me, then Mum would rush home to take care of her.

That flying-bomb scare made Mum rush out of the house half hysterical, wondering where the bomb had dropped. With all the dust around, and pavement stones or coal-cellar tops scattered around the street, she thought the bomb might have fallen on our school. You can imagine her fright.

Next thing we knew Mum came rushing into the school, often faster than other mothers, just to make sure we were O.K. Actually, most times we'd be comfortable in the air-raid shelter.

When Mum got off a bus near Paddington Station, coming home from work, she had nearly a mile to walk over a bridge and she'd be looking up for those flying-bombs that buzzed over with a flame shooting out of the tail. When the engine stopped everyone ducked because the bomb dived. It gave you a few seconds' warning.

Mum would be so sure the bomb was about to drop on our house that she'd start rushing home like she was going to catch it in her arms to save us. Like I said—the kids always come first. All mums are unselfish. Sometimes I wished they could become fight managers—though I certainly ain't gonna complain about my managers.

With the war going great guns and us ducking a bomb or two I suppose we kids felt the need for some action of our own. I can't say I was born to fight because of hunger, because I had parents that made sure I never starved. Hard times, yes. But we were never in rags or cadging for a crust. And Dad, though he had to know how to use his fists, wasn't exactly a big-time fighter or anything. But he considered it handy for me to know how to use the ole mitts.

Because I happened to be the senior of my section of the family it was always 'See our Tel' when kids in the neighbourhood started cutting up rough with the Downeses. Maybe some kids would have a go at one of the cousins down at the swimming baths or on a street corner, and he'd come running for me like I'm King Kong or something. I'm only nine or ten, but they've made me the big boy.

I tumbled that I got more whackings trying to take the cousins' part than any scraps I sorted out for myself. It was ridiculous. I was no tougher than anyone else, but the law of averages gave me my whack of wins.

I was potty about anything athletic, but nobody had bunged me a pair of boxing gloves from the cradle, like some kids get. I talked about boxing like every other kid, but never really fancied myself as a fighter. But the urge soon came.

At St. Saviour's School a teacher, Mr. Beal, was always nagging me about how good my cousin Ronnie Grogan could fight. Ronnie was under Beal before me and though he was away in the Navy the teacher kept saying, 'Now there was a boy who could box, Downes; he wouldn't stand for the other lads pushing him around.' Ronnie became a useful pro. So after school Beal used to keep a few boys behind in a little room and get the gloves out. I got lumbered. It wasn't that I was quick-tempered—I still ain't—but I just had to prove I was as good as the next geezer.

Of course, when Dad found out I was messing about with this boxing caper he did what a million dads do and stripped the kitchen floor, got down on his knees, and made me fight him. Sister Sylvie used to get frightened Dad would do his nut trying to sort me out, and she'd leave the room. Mum used to be worried stiff that I'd go a bit strong, even at that age, and end up getting a real clump behind the ear.

Anyway, truth is I nearly always ended up crying because I couldn't hit Dad. It wasn't temper, but sheer frustration. Then I knew I had to learn something about this boxing lark. I'd have to catch up with him sooner or later.

This new interest, and reading all the papers about the big names in boxing, killed any ideas of education. I wasn't exactly an Einstein at school but I wasn't dumb either. I failed the 11-plus exam, naturally, but I usually got up among the top ten in the class. Even then I had an eye on making the ratings. But to me going to a bigger school and wearing a badge and blazer, carrying a satchel and all that business, was the worse thing I could imagine. The last thing I wanted was a school cap. When we saw kids all dressed up we used to have a right go at them, so I didn't want to be sorted out. Failing the exam didn't bother me. But I knew what I wanted and where I was going.

So when our little mob from St. Saviour's moved up to St. Augustine School, which was on the edge of Paddington, I was coming to the front a bit. Other schools sent their boys, so we were first-termers all about the same age. That was the time for weighing-up the situation, sorting out a few opponents —and I picked pretty good matches for myself them days— to become top dog. The Downeses were still pushing 'Our Tel' up front.

The first week was right nervy. I'd look around fancying certain kids for a fight and saying to myself, 'He's only got to say something at playtime and he'll get a whack,' and the other kids were saying the same. We had some punch-ups until things got sorted out after a week or so and I knew who to fight and who not to fight.

I didn't need a manager. I never went mad and sorted out too many above my weight. But when you went to that kind of school seeing who got the caning first from the teacher was a bit of feat. It was seeing who was jack-the-lad. Of course, I got some regular canings.

Boxing with rules still hadn't really caught on with me. The school was sport-minded, but it was only when, maybe, the football was rained off, that they shoved us all in the hall, put a few benches around for a square, and got us pairing off for boxing.

Suddenly our teacher starts getting all enthusiastic (dead game he was!) and proudly sticks us in the national schoolboy championships. I'm half resisting at the time. We had a smashing little boxer in the school called Charlie Canavan and we used to move around together, but he could bang real good. I remember copping a right-hander off him and saying to myself, 'I hope he's not going to do that again.'

So I goes home and informs Dad that they've bunged me in the big school boxing. Kids from all over the country were entering and, believe me, the standard is high. Some of those kids are real crackers. Well, Dad has never boosted me or gone overboard about anything. He plays it cool. He'd rather have a go at me than pat my back. So when you get even the tiniest compliment I know I've done a feat.

'Boxing?' he says. 'You'll get a going over if you're not careful. You'll have to join a club and learn something.' Right away that becomes a challenge. 'Go down to Senior Street Club,' he says.

I told him that a kid in my class (Canavan) was going to Pembroke Boxing Club in North Kensington and I fancied going with him. 'Do what you like,' he says, 'but learn something.'

We used to take the Underground—we call it Tube—two or three times every week. Here I met a nice man, Charlie Powling, who was instructing. We struck up a friendship.

But when you're thirteen you start feeling a bit of a boy-about-town and, though I liked keeping fit, I didn't have any big ideas about boxing. I wanted to career around with the chaps, have a giggle at the pictures, maybe have a crafty date with the schoolgirl talent.

But all of a sudden Dad pressures me. 'Up the club, you,' he says; 'get the bag packed and get training.' So now I'm dragging back and forth whether I'm keen or not. And, worse ways, I gotta go through a third degree every time I come home.

'What'dya do tonight?' Dad would ask. Now he knows you do the same things at boxing clubs, but he's gotta make it a quiz. 'I boxed, I punched the bag, I skipped,' I'd say. 'So who was there?' he'd wanna know. I knew he didn't know a single kid at the club, so I'd answer 'Oh, Bill, Harry, Joe.' But you couldn't quieten Dad. He'd persist. 'What kinda boy is Joe?' he'd demand. 'He's big,' I'd say, 'but he can't punch much.' And so the rigmarole would go on.

Then comes my first real fight. I'm weighing around 6 st. 8 lb. and the qualifying stage of the schoolboy championships is held at Senior Street School. The teacher wants to take good care of his prize-fighters, so he sends us home early and we bunch up and go to my place. Of course, the family wanna know what this is all about.

'Well, you have to eat early cos you can't fight on a loaded stomach,' I'd say, like we're gonna get a special dish. I think we upset the home routine, so we finished up with spaghetti-on-toast and went off like a bunch of budding champs for the big night.

I don't mind admitting that I used to turn as white as a sheet and even feel a bit sick. Dad's looking at me like I'm gonna faint. Yet I wasn't nervous. But winning mattered and I suppose I worked myself up to a pitch. I went in banging, with a fair bit of craft, and stopped the first rival in a round and the second in three rounds.

Now I'm feeling ten feet tall, champ of Paddington. Don't say a word out of place, mate, or I'll very likely whack you, was the way I felt. But fighting to rule started to cure me of fighting without gloves. The satisfaction of knowing I could hold my own was enough.

The next day in school we gathered in the assembly hall and a teacher announced we'd got a couple of champions of Paddington and I felt right proud. But I was a bit bashful them days and I'm ducking me nut half hiding behind a bigger kid. But that little title meant as much to me then as winning the world title.

The teacher gives me and Canavan a big boost and tells the school he expects them to support us when we go for the next stage of the championships at Chelsea Barracks. I won there, too.

Now I'm really a big-time merchant. The clarion-call goes out to the family and a load of aunts and uncles turn up when North London has to box off with South London at the Polytechnic in Camden Town. I don't know it then, but this is a good excuse for the Downeses to get together for a booze-up after the boxing.

I lick a kid called Smart and we're all marching home laughing. Next on the list is Lime Grove Baths, which is nearer the Downeses' homes, and they're out in force for this one. I'm matched with a kid called Grout, but when I get there I find out he ain't fighting and they've put me in with a sub-stitute called Hillier.

I'm thinking: 'Hello, this is handy. What's all this about?'
And I soon find out. This Hillier knocks the life out of me for
two rounds. He's buzzing round picking off punches like a
world-beater and I'm thinking that if he's only a substitute
what would the first kid have done to me?

I manage to pile in and put a few punches on him in the
last round, but he gets the decision—and I taste the first
defeat. I'm really choked. Then someone shoves a schoolboy
manual under my nose and this Hillier kid is only posing for
the instruction pictures. He's a right schoolboy wonder, been
boxing for years. So I'm not feeling so bad about it. He went
on to become British champion.

But punching in the schoolboy championships didn't win
me a thing. They don't even give me a piece of paper to show
off. And Canavan brings a medal with a boxer on it to school
and we're all admiring it. I'm dying to get me a medal. So
down at Pembroke Club they make a coupla matches for me
and after I win they lead me to the prizes table. 'O.K., son,
what'dya want?' they said. 'I gotta have a medal,' I appealed.
'No medals, son.'

I wind up with a little china teapot for the first prize of my
life. Mum reckoned it was lovely and we've still got it. The
family have even carted it back and forth from America. We
wouldn't part with it.

Another time I remember bowling in the front door, proud
as a peacock, and without saying a word tossed a bronze medal
on the kitchen table. Mum looked pleased enough, but Dad
only half nodded in his begrudging kind of way to say 'Well
done'. It was enough for me. Championship of the world here
I come.

A year later I'm shaping better and getting bigger at 7 st.
12 lb. And some of the kids, I think, are frightened off by my
fancy pants. They were vivid scarlet satin boxer-swimming
trunks sent from the States by my sister Sylvie. Mum had
posted her a few local-paper clippings and she'd decided to
encourage me.

Sylvie and me were real close. Being two years older, she'd
come among the boys and clip a few ears if they started sorting

me out. 'Cause she knew they weren't gonna throw any punches, so she'd let 'em have it.

It was Sylvie's adventure in America that patterned my career—by accident.

From school she became a fair little dancer, and when she's twelve Mum spots an advert in the paper for recruits for 'Terry's Juveniles', which was a big act for kids. Sylvie gets taken on and before we know it she's playing in pantomimes in the West End, touring the provinces, and growing into a pretty good acrobat. This is the career she wants. But she can't stay a tiddler all her life and Dad's punting around considering where he can place her and spots an advert for circus work.

An Australian agent, Digger Pugh, wants girls for Tom Arnold's big London circus. So Sylvie gives me a bodyguard job. She's having an audition with this Digger geezer on a Sunday and says I should go along.

I mean, at fourteen, I must be Mr. Big or something. Anyway, when we meet Pugh he starts asking what I'm gonna do for a living and I say 'Become a boxer'. That does it. This Pugh has been a pretty good boxer himself and starts getting out the scrapbooks, and we're chatting like good 'uns while poor old Sylvie is still looking on.

I'm real impressed with this guy and Sylvie's breaking her neck doing a spin or a backbend and we're chatting away about boxing. He's well satisfied with Sylvie and takes us home in his car, a smashing Jaguar, brand new, bright red, which he'd brought from the States. I'm thinking the sun shines out of his eyes.

I've only ever ridden in the old bangers that Dad's probably bought and sold for a score of quids. So Sylvie signs up and she's working with the circus at Harringay Arena—later to be the scene of my first paid fight.

Every night I got the bodyguard job, so bird-chasing is out for me. I have to wait outside the station for Sylvie after each circus performance and just to keep me on my toes I'm pulling at two greyhounds. Dad's training himself greyhounds like we're gonna win a family fortune. 'Keep them dogs moving all the time,' he'd say as I plodded, come rain or shine, to the station.

I'd be ducking and diving with the dogs as the crowds came off the trains with me searching for Sylvie. Dad would argue it kept me on my toes for the fight game. Gave me stamina, he reckoned. Sylvie's working good with a web act—doing kick-outs from a high rope and all that—and chatting the other girls who've been on tour in America. It was all romantic to her.

She plucked up courage to ask Mum and Dad if she could go with a circus in the States. They soon turned her down. But she was smart bringing her mates home to tea and getting them chatting favourably about life in the States and how you could pick up a bob or two besides get marvellous circus experience.

So, bang, Sylvie gets permission to go. She joins the famous Ringling Brothers and circuits from New York to Baltimore, Philadelphia, Washington, and everywhere. She first goes to Ringling Brothers' winter camp in Sarasota, Florida, where training begins for the tour.

For all the fighting dream spots—Sylvie beats me to the punch. She appears at Madison Square Garden, New York, and Boston Garden, where I later fought twice for the middle-weight championship of the world

The American tour has shaped Sylvie into a young woman and an artist. She came back to London appearing at Harringay and I'm back in the old routine as the brother-in-charge complete with the exercise-the-dogs routine at the station every night. The dogs are different but the results are the same. There's more good losers among 'em. Honest, I'm fit enough then to drop the leads and run away from these grey-hounds. They couldn't even catch me.

Sylvie is like me, fired with ambition. I can't stand people who just sit around content with their lot. I love those 'ave-a-go merchants. While I'm traipsing around with the dogs, training like a dog at my club, building up frame and stamina, Sylvie convinces Mum and Dad she's favourite to go back to America again.

With Sylvie working hard for fame in the States there comes a customary Cockney family bust-up at home. A bit of a bull-and-a-cow we call it—a row. I suppose Mum gets a bit cheesed off with the old man blowing his cash at the dogs or something and she decides we're leaving Paddington—and him.

Dad's had everything from rag to junk shops, garages, been a bus-driver, mechanic—anything better than working to hours. He was a good mechanic, too. But you gotta have a regular wage coming in, otherwise women get a bit fed-up. Mum creeps over to Catford, in South London, looking for an old friend to stay with, but she'd moved. Me, I'm fourteen and become the big minder once more. Can't leave Mum, can I? But I know we're much better off being home with Dad. Anyway, next thing I know we're off to Taunton, in Somerset, and I'm choked with no idea why we've sorted out Somerset to hide. Me, the big guy from the Smoke, messing around with all those country yokels. But I soon discovered they're tough too.

I suppose I'm bouncing about Taunton with a right chip on my shoulder being away from London. All the kids are coming around and asking questions about living in town. Mum's out working, and the ridiculous thing about this move is that Sylvie, who could be anywhere from the Ringling Brothers' camp at Florida to shows in New York, Washington, or the West Coast, is the go-between with letters from Mum and Dad.

He can't understand why some of the family haven't found out where we're living. If we're in London the Downeses would soon pass the word. But this trip to Taunton has fooled him. He's writing off to Sylvie saying it's ridiculous us breaking up over nothing, and Mum's writing back saying she's fed-up, and poor ole Sylvie is trying to keep the peace with letters from 5,000 miles away which are taking a month to flow back and forth.

But it's three months that we're struggling down in Taunton and I get used to the accent. They didn't even start to understand me. But I sort out a few of the tougher guys as mates and when one of them gets a nice backhander off the teacher at school I'm right mad about it.

I stared at him, thinking to myself that the teacher's taken a right liberty, and that I'd like to see him try that whacking lark with me.

The teacher is no mug, he must have read my thoughts. He moved across the room to me and made some remark about getting on with my work. I suppose I'm looking at him a bit flash, or something, so he accompanied this order with a nice whack across the ear. Having already made up my mind I wasn't going to stand for none of that punch-up stuff I automatically shot up in the seat.

It was then I learned it was smarter to stay put. I must have been half shaping up, but before I know it the teacher, an elderly but big, strong guy, shot an uppercut at me that smashed straight in the mouth. I don't have any respect for him—but I learned respect there and then for the uppercut punch.

The blood spurts out and little do I know that it's the taste of things to come. The teacher says to wash the mouth out, or something. I'm saying, 'Yea, what's left of it,' and the blood is dripping all over me. I go home trying to check the bleeding but realize the lip is cut clean through. It's a beauty of a gash.

Mum is out working and the woman we're living with insists I go off to hospital. I suppose it was then I really knew I was going to be a fighter. Because when the doctor starts stitching the lip—about eight stitches it was—I'm appealing to him to do a nice job cos I'm a boxer and I don't want it to open again.

Ever since I've been making those appeals when doctors have got me in stitches.

I carry the lip-scar around as a reminder of the punch I should have ducked. It has defiantly survived the ring wars. And while everyone else considers it just another Terry Downes trade-mark I don't want to disillusion them that it's a souvenir for talking out of turn to a teacher in Taunton.

Mum goes mad when she sees the damage and I said I got it for nothing, but the next thing I know she's making an assault charge against the teacher. The cops are buzzing around and statements are being prepared and they sort of hint that the teacher reckoned I was about to wallop him, so Mum decides to drop it. It's the first and only time Terry Downes has to swallow it—and loses by retirement.

They Called me a Limey Licker

AT THIS stage of my life I'm fearing I'll grow up a country bumpkin, and nothing worse could happen to a townie like me. (Now I know the swede-bashers, the guys from the sticks, the lucky ones who sniff all that free fresh air up their hooter, are really the smart ones!)

But, bang, next thing I know, Dad—God bless him!—has rolled up in a big lorry, big reunion, and we're back in Paddington where we belong.

His influence again had me slogging away at the fight-training. Pembroke Club and Charlie Powling were pleased to see me back and I got into the old routine. But, naturally, I've got to earn a crust, so my cousins Bob and Cyril put me to work cleaning cars, greasing-up, and what-not with their little business in Harrow Road, Paddington. I'm out all weathers with that cold water, scrubbing the hire cars they owned. Couldn't expect any favours, like, being a relation, so had to pitch in.

But even at fifteen I regarded daily work as a mere filler-in. My ambition was to train hard enough to become a champion, earn some real money, and invest. Fighting was the only real talent I had. I had to gamble whether or not to concentrate on the fighting career. I suppose I could have wound up with whackings and nothing to show for it, but that's a fair gamble you have to take.

It's all very well for people knocking boxing and pointing out the pitfalls. They shouldn't underestimate the modern fighter. We know there are dangers, but so very few boys today take the kind of hidings that will seriously harm them.

Where could a guy like me, without the chance of higher

education, from a rough-and-ready family, have got the chance to make myself a pretty fair business man? No false modesty with me. I fought hard and worked hard and I'm comfortable —all right, well off—for the rest of my life—I hope!

So I've got a few scars to show for it. Brother, you can walk into any pub, in any town, pick up somebody else's beer, say a word out of place, and maybe you'll end up getting a busted nose—for nothing! Think of those miners who wind up with lung diseases and dozens of other jobs with occupational hazards. There's nothing like the fight business for a boy from a working-class background to make some real money.

I knew these things as a kid and planned my career. I wasn't an overnight wonder. It took years of sweat, blood, and toil (I've heard that before) and, like Jack Benny, it took ten years to make me an overnight star.

Jumping from schoolboy to A.B.A. Youth Championships is quite a step, because the opposition has grown stronger and smarter. Junior boxing in Britain is at a high level. Some of the kids are brilliant.

In the London Youth semi-final I was drawn against a smart kid called Davis, who had beaten me, as a schoolboy, the previous year. It looked a right bad draw. But I'd learned a bit and steamed straight in to beat Davis pretty easy this time. I got out of the ring and stayed to watch the boy I'm gonna face in the final. It's a tricky Tottenham geezer named Brian Jago. He could move around and catch punches cleverly and whack pretty good, too.

I weighed this match up that I'd have to start punching to the body and weaken him—and it worked. We had a good little battle and I got the points. I was London champion and had made the discovery that body-whacking pays off. It was that three-round match that helped create my boxing bodywork. A few years later Jago was one of my stable-mates as a pro.

The London final qualified me for the Great Britain event and the semi-finals were held at Manor Place Baths, in Walworth, a good and tough district.

I'm matched with Terry Tulley, of Brighton (he became a pro), and we have a real good punch-up in the afternoon semi-final. I won. The finals, the same evening, are at the Albert Hall and I reckon the first fight might have taken a bit of steam out of me. My opponent for the title—to us a really big title and tough to win—was Harry Edwards, from Birmingham. He'd been lucky enough to get a bye and was fresher than me.

Anyway, sad to say that T. R. Downes, the fire-eater from Paddington, slipped up for his first big night in the famous hall where Gigli used to sing and where champions from Kid Lewis to Carnera appeared. Harry boy nicked the final verdict. He, too, turned pro and was going well as a light-weight when a suspected heart murmur blocked his career. But in February 1964 Harry got the all-clear for a come-back and I had to turn up to cheer him on.

I hadn't realized the Youth final would be my last fight for some years in England.

I don't mind a bit of hard work, but I was knocking the hands up a bit getting under cars, serving petrol, grafting at all odd hours that interfered with training. So I moved on to a car showroom, S. Morris & Co., in Edgware Road, standing around in a white coat with a feather duster. Blimey, it was the finest thing that could happen to me. A right doddle it was. Better than office work and nice regular hours.

Then, with a shocking suddenness, the pattern of my life was changed. On a Saturday afternoon, June 7, 1952, a telegram was delivered to our house, 162 Westbourne Terrace. I don't remember ever having seen a telegram before. I just nodded to the kid who brought it and, being on my own, wondered what the hell I should do. It was just addressed 'Downes', so I ripped the envelope open.

The telegram read: *Sylvia in bus accident lost right arm above elbow. Mercy Hospital, Baltimore, Maryland. Our legal department making arrangements for attorney to represent Sylvia. Everything possible being done for her. Signed: Ringling Circus.*

I just sagged at the knees and sobbed. The shock was so great I failed to grasp its real meaning. Sylvie, only eighteen, being featured in an act billed as 'Abbott Sisters—Daring Aerialists' had lost her right arm. It was the sort of tragedy I'd heard about in wartime. It seemed unbelievable such a terrible thing could strike a young girl—the sister I loved.

I waited for Mum and Dad to return, and already the news had been printed in the London papers and Dad had been shown the story. We hadn't realized that June 6 had become D-Day for the Downes family. On our sideboard was Sylvie's last letter home. It said: *Mum, you mustn't worry if you don't hear from me as regularly as you would like. There's nothing to worry about. Nothing can ever happen to me.*

Reporters came to us and their advice helped Mum how to apply for a special passport and visa. Our only concern was getting Mum off to America—to her it seemed like flying to another world—and comforting Sylvie. 'I must go to her,' was all Mum could say. The passport office and the American Embassy were both co-operative. B.O.A.C. guaranteed Mum a seat on the next plane—price £96. Getting the money wasn't easy, but a whip-round, pawning her wedding-ring, and borrowing the rest, got Mum off.

Sylvie's circus, appearing at Lawrence Park, Baltimore, had to move on within twenty-four hours of the accident. The show must go on and all that jazz. The lonely English girl was practically adopted by the Baltimore people. They were warm, wonderful people.

Sylvie had been riding in the mid-window seat of a No. 23 bus, with four other girls of her act: Brenda Goring, aged nineteen, Evelyn Kent, eighteen, Margaret Smith, twenty-one, and Gladys Rimmer, twenty. All were Cockneys and had performed in London. The bus was taking them to the circus site. As the bus crossed the main street, at the corner of Lexington and Liberty Street, the mere twenty-two-year-old driver, Roy Farmer, accidently caught the rear of the bus against the kerb. Because of the fierce ninety-odd-degree heat, windows were wound completely down and Sylvie was resting part of her arm on the window-ledge.

At the corner was a steel telephone or utility pole. The bus tipped against it and Sylvie's arm was crushed between pole and the metal side of the bus. It dangled, said witnesses, as though holding by a thread. Sylvie screamed, Brenda Goring fainted, a man watching on the sidewalk fainted, too.

C

Sylvie, I was told later, calmly pulled her arm inside and rested it on her lap. Her life was then virtually saved by two Baltimore policemen. I gratefully print their names in capitals because I never want to forget them. Patrolman JOHN SINNOTT, who had been directing traffic at the intersection, tried to apply a tourniquet with his handkerchief until the arrival of another patrolman, BILL CLAYTON, who took off his belt to put on a stronger tourniquet and stop Sylvie bleeding to death.

They were staggered by Sylvie's show of guts. We were so proud of her when everybody told us how brave she had been. They rushed her off to Mercy Hospital for the amputation. There was no chance of saving the arm. What was so diabolically upsetting was that policemen—including Sinnott and Clayton—had previously reported the danger of the corner-pole with buses taking the sharp corner. The kerb, they had protested, was too close to the pole. There had been three earlier accidents, though not so severe as Sylvie's.

And the driver, though I don't blame him, was fined $25 for reckless driving. He had also exceeded his eight-hour stint taking the bus on the tripper route to the circus. Later, Sylvie's claim against the company was settled out of court and the pole was taken down.

There was an outcry in Baltimore, and sympathy from the people, who overcame us with their generosity. I soon found out the English, including me, had weighed-up the Yanks all wrong. We're often having a go at them because they're loud. We say they're rude. Please and thanks don't come so natural to them. But this is just a natural way of life, the same as our odd-ball habits shock them. Sure, they nearly all play at being tough guys, they're not so reserved as the English—don't look at me!—and though they speak the same language I know people here often resent American brashness. I suppose because it's a country born by violence it's stayed that way. But let me make it real clear. There's nothing wrong with America. And if you'd had the tretament they gave my sister —and me—you'd think they were the greatest people in the world. For me I can find more rights than wrong with them. After all, we English ain't all angels. I'll bet we had to hand out a nice few whackings to keep our Empire in order in the old days.

Anyway, with Mum a bunch of nerves and wondering how Sylvie would take this lousy accident, she arrived in Baltimore without knowing a soul to console her. Mum rushed to the Mercy Hospital, where she got such a friendly reception, and they lead her to Sylvie's room. Mum had to stop for a second outside, making sure she held back any tears, and ready to put on the smile.

Suddenly she heard music coming from Sylvie's room. Sylvie's nuts on music. The neighbours in Paddington used to watch her dancing around, even during the air-raids, and all said she's born to be a dancer.

The hospital room door was about a foot from the ground, and Mum could see somebody dancing around in slippers. She shoved the door open—and it's Sylvie! What a girl! Only three days after the accident and she's hamming-it-up dancing around. But you can imagine the tonic that gave my mum. Right away she decided that Sylvie must have the family with her. Dad must pack up the bus-driving and I had to forget all about fighting and garage-working. We're on our way to the States. We hustled around scraping up enough fare to make the passage by tramp steamer—but we made it.

Dad and I stepped on the dock at New York and Mum and Sylvie were there to meet us. I'm a hard-hearted geezer, being a fighter, but I don't mind admitting I had a right good cry. It was some moment for me. We four were together again. But before I could say 'Sugar Ray Robinson' Sylvie was back with the circus, despite the accident, working in the production numbers.

Strangers in a strange country, honest grafters but without a serious trade. That was the Downes lot. But we turned into big-shots in one hit. A well-known society woman, a Mrs. Pennyman—and I still haven't met her!—told Mum she planned a holiday in Europe and we could take over her house.

This handsome house, with all the contents, the beautiful silverware and everything, was ours. Mrs. Pennyman merely locked off one little room just for a few personal things, or something, but we've taken the rest. We lived like lords.

A fellah who used to visit Sylvie in hospital pops round and says he's been drafted and hands over his car! 'You might as well keep this,' he said. It's one of the few times in my life I'm stuck for words. I mean, how marvellous can people get? I haven't got a driving licence 'cos I'm only sixteen but knocking around with Dad's old bangers for years has made me a pretty good driver just the same.

So I ran around in the old Chevrolet as proud as punch. To me it was like having a Rolls-Royce. Meanwhile, Mum was often invited out and she got special friendship from a Mrs. Isobel Graham-Hughes, who was a friend of the Duchess of Windsor. Before the Duke made the match with the then Mrs. Simpson she lived in Biddle Street, Baltimore, where Mum used to have these tea parties with Mrs. Graham-Hughes. And they still correspond.

It was all this friendly encouragement, with Sylvie the sweetheart of the city, that helped her recover. The papers practically adopted her. Strangers would stop us in the street and ask how she was getting along. Life was lush for us Limeys. Then somebody spoiled it, suggesting I went to school!

Leave orf, me going to school with a lot of Yanks who couldn't understand a word I was saying. I should think so. So I soon looked around for a job. I wasn't exactly an Hemingway, but I always reckoned that the newspaper lark wasn't a bad game. Sylvie, with plenty of front, had been telling the locals about her young brother who was a bit of a boxing star in London. Kids in the States rarely put on gloves until they're about sixteen. and I'm almost a veteran at that age. Hold your breath—I was even offered a scholarship at Michigan University!

Guys like Canavan, Davis, Jago, Edwards really knew the game compared to the American kids. I had nothing to fear. So I had no bother getting my first job as a copy-boy on the *Baltimore News-Post*, and I'm telling you I spoke to every employee in the building within a week.

Everyone in the joint wanted to hear the Limey speak. They sent me on errands that I don't even understand, like paper-curlers or back-arm stretchers, but I loved it. I think maybe they think all Englishmen are educated at 'Arrer, I mean Harrow, and they like listening to my Cockney chat because it comforted them. But the paper was good to me. Whenever I go back to Baltimore they treat me like the prodigal son.

It must be quite a town, because Sylvie still lives there. And she's happily married, had four marvellous kids, and the way she overcomes the handicap of a lost arm has to be seen to be believed. She puts the little girls curlers on without any help, and does everything in the house. Blimey, there's been plenty of times when I wished my left hand was as good as hers!

Having settled in, I figured I'd get in some sort of fighting shape, so went down to the local Y.M.C.A. Let me make it clear that the Y.M.C.A. in the States is a big deal with, maybe, property covering a whole block. The facilities make most British clubs look like mouse-traps. It's a terrific organization. I packed up my little bag of gear and a bit shyly (honest!) I reported for a work-out.

A trainer named Lee Halfpenny gave me the low-down and said he wanted to take a look at me boxing. I'm weighing around 132 lb., a scrawny feather-weight, and the only guy available was a nifty-looking light-middle of maybe 153 lb. To me the bigger they are the harder they fall, so we put the gloves on and I stuck out plenty of fancy left jabs, doing a bit of showing-off, and this Halfpenny geezer called in the rest of the guys.

'Marvellous,' he kept saying. Like I said, at home I'm just a pretty fair performer, but over there I'm getting the rave treatment, the lap-up. This geezer I moved around with was the state champion, called Jimmy Hines. A smart boxer, not too much of a puncher, but he knew the business. Right away they offer me a year's free membership of the Y.M.C.A.

I'm so pleased about it I insist this Hines geezer came to our house to tea. Next thing I know he married Sylvie. It's about the best match I've ever made.

So now the club entered me in a novice competition and we have to creep outside the city for this tournament. The guy I'm fighting is also a novice, but when I see him it frightens the life out of me. My life, he's a negro with moustache and beard, and muscles growing out of his muscles. I'm used to having a punch-up with skinny white kids and I ain't fancying this geezer too much.

I'm so terrified I darted out of the corner thinking if I don't nail this geezer a bit quick he'll very likely murder me. It's with fear more than hope that I start throwing dozens of punches. And, what dya know? I stop him in under two rounds. What a relief that was.

Now I'm entered in the state championship, novice class, and I go through that lot like a dose of salts. All that London club-battling had paid off. So the Y.M.C.A. put me in the bigger championship, called the South Atlantic, which involves other states, like Virginia and Washington, and some Service camps.

The *Baltimore News-Post* is playing-up the fighting and the critics are saying that this Limey Licker is liable to find the open class a lot tougher, and all that. I'm reading every line and in those days I'm believing every word of it.

I say this because writers everywhere should realize they have a responsibility and that kids are very impressionable at that age. Words can hurt. Lucky I learned to live with criticism later. That's the advantage of being thick-skinned around the nut! And I also found out not to believe everything I read, because there are writers, I think, who know about writing but little about fighting. And since fighting became my business I spent a lot of time at it. That's what makes me give opinions that often differ from the writers. I'm not as obstinate guy and I hope I'm always willing to learn, but I can count the writers on one hand whose opinions really count with me.

If I'd listened to them all I'd have been retired years ago, without even winning a world title, and very likely skint. Tom Phillips, then with the *Daily Herald*, said I should retire *before* I went on to win the world crown, had three world-title fights, and I finished up with a fourth shot. How wrong can you get?

I just wish all writers would get out of this habit of writing-off a boxer because of one defeat. Did anyone write-off Dempsey or Louis when they were both knocked out long before they became world heavy-weight champions?

I made up my mind pretty young that there were just as many mugs among newspapermen as there were among us fighters. Yet it was publicity and, to some extent, newspaper support that got me to the top. Fighters can't survive without it.

Getting the build-up at sixteen made me a bit of a big-shot. I'd fight anyone. Now I know it's a good job I didn't, because I'd have finished up rocking and reeling. My name went forward for the National Championships being held in Boston in 1952 and I'm training like a b—— and figuring I can win. But Lee Halfpenny is no mug. 'At sixteen,' he said. 'you can go in there with older guys and get the hell punched outa yer. We'll leave it to next year and then you'll win it.'

Me, pulling out of a fight? What kind of a deal is this? But, like I said, I'm not mug enough not to listen and, of course, Lee was right. When I hear fathers of good juniors bragging about the number of fights the kids have had I always feel like saying, 'So what are you doing, boasting or apologizing?' Good boy boxers, I discovered, rarely last to become good men fighters. Either their fathers or trainers get too brave.

Next, the Y.M.C.A. mob, which is a bright boxing lot, were invited to take on the Marines at Quantico, Virginia, camp. This looked a right challenge for me and I was bucked about it. So off we went and they tell me I'm fighting a guy called Harold Conklin. He's got a name to suit my nose, I thought, and with a moniker like that he can't be much of a fighter. Just shows how wrong you can be. Me and Harold had a right hard punch-up, terrific match it was, but he got the points. It was my first defeat over there, but I wasn't down-hearted because I always knew where I was going, and this Conklin character was Inter-Service champion and talk of the camp.

Me and a guy named Elwood Myers were the only white fighters on our team. Myers, who was a light-heavy-weight, lived outside Baltimore, so we called him 'Country'. He reminded me a lot of Rocky Marciano, being a right hard nut and always knocking 'em out. He won, in style, at Quantico and, since we were mates, a Marine major sorted us both out for a chat.

'If you consider joining the Marines,' he says, 'after you've done the initial boot-training let me know and I'll make sure that you guys are transferred to this camp and you'll get on the boxing team with passes to Baltimore every week-end. Life is luxury in the Marines when you're on the boxing squad. I'd like you guys to join us.'

It's all very flattering, I'm thinking, but I don't plan to be doing any fighting for real.

The next boxing trip takes us to the Convention Hall, Atlantic City, a seaside resort where Joey Giardello, whom I later licked at Wembley, shocked everyone (except me) winning the world middle-weight title from Dick Tiger in 1963. A big convention is going on in the town, and I'm well pleased looking around the prize table and spotting a TV set for the winners, with a radio for the losers.

Now this is something worth winning. I'd heard about the amateur kids around New York who'd always boxed for the same prize, a rusted silver watch, which they took and regularly handed back for a few dollars under the table. I always fancied being the awkward guy who could louse up the whole works by wanting to keep the watch!

A TV set seemed a right luxury to me. I'm matched against a dapper Italian guy, Mickey Rosette, and I weighed him up with great expectations, but when the bell sounded he came out standing southpaw. I can't stand those cack-handers. It's the first time I even saw a southpaw in the States and it turned out he's the last but one I fought there.

While I'm fathoming out this hip-switch lark, wallop! he's hit me a corker of a punch and I'm on the floor! It's the first time I'd been down in my life and I'm thinking this is not only a liberty but a diabolical one. I'm right choked and a bit embarrassed in the bargain. Anyway, I got up and we're banging away again like lunatics but it's no use, I just couldn't handle the wrong-foot-forward game.

This little 'Dago' does me up. It's a terrific fight, but he

pips me for the verdict. And when I see the difference in the
prizes I was right fed-up. I lugged this little radio out and my
mate 'Country' Myers, with his big wallop, flattened some
poor geezer and went home with a handsome TV set.

Anyway, it don't take me long to learn that I've got to train
to handle all styles. I don't show-off or nothing when I'm
beaten. It's just that I get sort of annoyed with myself for
standing for some of the punches I can see coming.

So I get back to training in the gym again. I'm not chasing
the birds—or broads, as they say in the States—because I
live for this boxing lark. And I'm enjoying the newspaper
work, though I can't say I'm taking it too seriously. I don't
figure to become editor.

To my surprise, 'Country' Myers, who's apparently had a
bit of bother at home, rolls up and says he's joining the Marines.
The major at Quantico had conned him. I liked Myers. Some
week-ends I used to creep down to his little farm and help his
old man killing off the beef and we'd become good mates.

So now I'm thinking if 'Country' is leaving I might as well
go with him. After all, I'll soon be eligible for U.S. Service
draft, but because Uncle Sam figures most kids are at school
at seventeen they don't want to nick them while they're
studying so the draft usually comes around twenty-one or
twenty-two. Now this is no game for me. I figured I'll be
looking for a nice few quid fighting at that age, not laying
about in the Army stationed out of nowhere.

'Country' is booked for boot-camp training on December 6,
1953, and I work it out that though I'll have to do an extra
year, making it three years, I'd be better off volunteering for
the Marines and getting out when I was twenty. Besides, with
all the bull the major had given us I reckoned I'd get plenty of
boxing experience and be near home at the same time. Yes,
that would do me. So I tried to nip down and enrol with
Myers's draft.

But his draft was full, or something, and they signed me on
for January 1954. . . . Gung Ho, Halls of Montezuma, here I
come.

Me in the U.S. Marines

HAVING figured out a dozen good reasons why I should volunteer for the U.S. Marines, a final clincher came when I learned you could get six weeks wages for joining up. That appealed to me. And when I heard I was going to Paris Island, South Carolina, it conjured up romantic notions like a beach at Hawaii. This was really living it up. But, brother, did I make a ricket! This Paris Island was worse than hell, bang in the middle of swamps.

A big Baltimore join-up campaign had conned about 100 geezers, besides me, to become glamorous Leathernecks, and on the train to camp we're all playing craps and chatting our load about being the crack Baltimore platoon, and all that jazz. Then we came to reality.

As the train doors opened and we ambled out on to the track, or platform, these Marine instructors are coming at us like fiends. They were yelling blue murder, clumping guys around the head, treating us like fodder, and I find I'm trying to reject the treatment. But it's a lost cause. You either swallow it and take the punishment or go through a bigger hell.

Geezers wearing one-stripe are demanding, 'Say sir to me,' and if you fancy letting 'em have a wallop they only bring two guys up to grab you and give you a good whacking. The barracks were modern, with good equipment, and compared to an army camp in England where I played football recently it was paradise. But the discipline was murderous. You honestly couldn't make a film of it and make it look bad enough to be true.

Two guys committed suicide while I was there, so that gives

you an idea of what we went through. You couldn't break out because you'd wind up sinking in a swamp. Everything was done in double-time running, which I didn't mind, because at least I was a fit kid. They stripped us off, we bundled up the civvy clothes and shipped them home. That was the last connection with humanity. This was going to be twelve weeks of torture. I'd have given that six weeks wages back with interest if I'd known.

They ran us off to the equipment centre, with a right hard-nut quartermaster, where we copped all our gear. They bathed and sprayed us with disinfectant, sheared every hair off the head, and I guarantee I did look tasty standing naked, with a bald bonce, while a sergeant shoved a soft fatigue hat on my head. They automatically put the peak over the eyes to force you to keep the head up and as I tried to push the hat back a bit somebody gave me a good whack.

I'm walking around in a right state trying to grab my uniform, can't see a bloody thing, double-timing it to barrack-room, collecting kitbag, carrying rifle, and being raced here, there, and everywhere. You're under constant supervision, with whacks being given out like trading stamps, and while I could stand the physical effort, I found the mental strain was ridiculous.

They even forced us to go to bed at the attention! They gave us, maybe, fifteen minutes each evening to write home on issue paper, and I managed a few lines every night before somebody yelled out, 'Beds, lights out.' I was lucky if I caught the post once a week.

It's so difficult to even relax with a chat. The smoke-breaks were short, and those guys who liked a puff were becoming nervous wrecks. When all the dashing about was finished, about five o'clock, I thought we could at least calm down. But out would come instruction books and questions about fire-arms and equipment. We didn't have the combat-training I'd expected—that came at another camp later—but solely mental-conditioning. You was just dirt until they drilled you long enough to be called a Marine. I had trouble even managing to chat the guy in the bunk above mine. They dragged us out of bed at 6 a.m., making us toe a bed-line, and we did look a choice sight. The only geezers who reckoned they left us in bed for a lay-in were those who were milkmen before they enlisted. The worse part, for me, was playing sentry nursemaid to the poor geezers whose nerves were so bad they couldn't stop wetting the bed. Some could have been 'working their ticket'; others were going off their nut. Anyway, the guy who got this fire-watch racket had to go around every hour waking up the culprits and insisting they went to the toilet!

The punishment came if one of the guys went on wetting when you were on duty.

We also had these psychological tests, playing around with kid's coloured bricks, matching them up and what-not. Being a tough guy didn't count if you couldn't fathom out these toys! Even Cassius Clay, a chatterbox who remembers his lines better than some actors, had trouble with this test. He got k.o.'d.

About a dozen recruits in my platoon got weeded out for one thing and another. But I stuck the marching game, and clumps around the head, pretty well. I got hardened to it and consoled myself that when I finished this lot—it must be tougher than prison—the major who chatted us in Quantico would be waiting to welcome me.

So every hour of the day I'm marching and galloping to shouts of 'Gung Ho!' and being rattled into action by the haunting Halls of Montezuma march. You can hear it all in your sleep. They are brain-washing to make you a robot Marine. It's enough to drive anyone potty.

Then I wrote off to the major at Quantico, casually mentioning that I was near passing-out from this boot-camp torture and ready for the fighting squad. You can imagine how filled in I was getting a curt reply saying the major had been posted to Korea! Here's a guy who is promising me near-home posting and he's been shoved abroad. So what chance me!

We rookies got to the stage of sweating on where we're being posted. I applied for Special Services, which includes anything athletic, and go on to North Carolina, Camp

Joining the Marines in 1956

With the US Marines boxing team in 1956

I get the best boxer award in Washington in March 1956

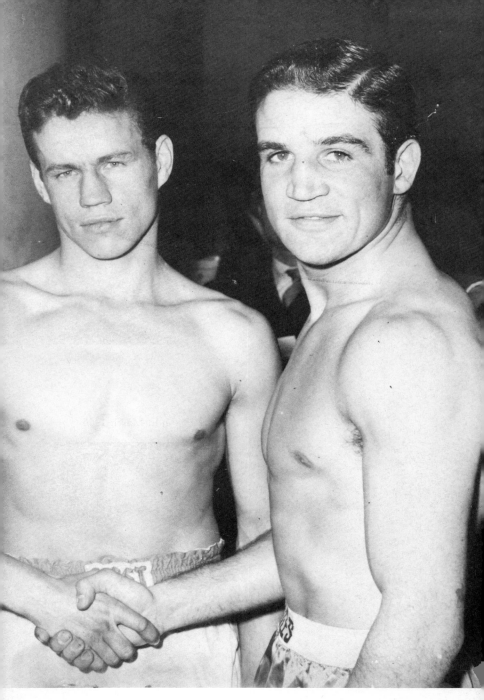

With Phil Edwards weighing in for
the British Middleweight Championship in September 1958

Ducking beneath a long searching left from the world middleweight
Champion, Paul Pender, in the title fight, Boston USA, January 1961

Lejeune, for the main combat-training. At last we're treated like real Marines, a tinge of respect, and we've got a little town to get a beer and, maybe, chance of a pass. I started shaping up like a Marine and fancied the life.

Having a bit of a roll-call, some tough-guy sergeant, the kind they just couldn't characterize for a film, calls out for the Jock Strappers—the slang for athletic squads. Big guys, some of them 7 ft. basketball players, line up with the baseball-bashers and other ball-game boys gradually fall into line. All of them are ordered to squat—and Marine T. R. Downes is left alone. I don't budge an eyelid.

'What the hell are you,' bawled this guff-voiced sergeant.

'I box,' I said.

'Say "Sir" at the start and finish,' he bellowed.

'Sir, I box, sir,' said I.

'Where the hell do you come from, you bum?' he demanded.

Saying, 'Sir, I'm from Baltimore, sir,' doesn't satisfy this tough nut.

'That ain't no Baltimore accent,' he bawls again.

'Sir, well, I'm really from England, sir,' I answered.

'You goddamn Limey son-of-a-bitch coming here giving me cheek, what the hell is this. You say you can fight? Can you whip me, Limey?'

'Sir, I don't really know, sir,' I said, weighing him up and realizing I'll have to spot him at least 2 st. if it comes to a punch-up, but I'm dying to have a go. He steps over to test my stomach by prodding it with a parade-stick. I'm sort of laughing, so the sergeant gives me a tasty little dig, and I automatically pull back, but because the other guys are sitting I tumble over them and it gave them all a good laugh.

'You goddamn Limeys can't take a punch,' he said, and this made me fighting mad to get at the flash git, weight or no weight advantage.

I'm back on my feet, without even thinking about any compulsory eight-count, and yelling: 'If you wanna fight me there's a ring over there. Come on, put 'em up or shut up.'

This is practically enough to have you strung up in the Marines for insubordination. But the sergeant, whose word is law, has got a better idea. He fancied getting me a nice good belting for everyone to see. 'Oh, wise guy, are you?' he said. 'Well, we've got a fighter in a squad who'll have a go at you, Limey. Then we'll see if you can fight.'

I calmed down and thought, 'This is nice, this guy sorting me out an opponent without chatting it over with me,' and was considering what kind of geezer I would get. I wasn't no Hercules at the time. I was a small light-weight, maybe around 9 st. 6 lb. I'd grown since the Y.M.C.A. days, but a lot of it was just puppy fat. But if you swallow it in the Marines you're dead. You've gotta be game.

When other guys get these sort of dust-ups with authority they scarper off to the padre and pour out their troubles or go to whatever aid they can. The padre and all of them had heard all this before. Me, I gotta punch it out and hope for the best.

But when they shoved me up against a squad of real tough negro fighters, the pick of the camp, I reckoned it would be better facing a firing-squad. Can't get myself a nice skinny geezer, maybe my size, they have to pair me off with an ebony-muscled fighter who must have outweighed me by 2 st.

Well, it was no use messing about, so I danced around all clever when I tumbled the geezer was just a big, strong mug. I let him have a good swing at me, ducked, and then jabbed out the old left. After he'd missed a bit he started tiring. So I planted a beauty of a punch into his belly and he folded up and went down like a good 'un. Good as gold he was laying there, knocked out. It was such a lovely sight.

That punch at least got me some respect, a few pats on the back, and even the sergeant seemed to start liking me. I got to like him back and though he didn't do me any favours we sorta under tood each other.

It's surprising how a show of strength in the Services brings buddies. I wasn't really much better at the fight lark then plenty of others, but all that London teaching, with the ole nifty footwork, fooled 'em.

Doing the regular soldiering, darting about with guns and all that rigmarole was at least what I'd expected, and I started settling down. It was no use moaning, was it? The camp had a P.X. store where you could buy brass cleaner, razor-blades, and all the essential gear. But they put the bar up to us buying Pogey Bait, which was bits of grub. They didn't mind the folks sending the odd parcel, with a bar of chocolate and some biscuits, but they wouldn't let you buy it on camp. You *had* to eat the Marine-cooked grub.

Guys used to go spare just for a bar of chocolate, and I soon discovered that you could get, maybe, as much as a dollar for a nickel bar of chocolate. So right away I declared myself in the black-market lark. I mean, I'd served a tasty apprenticeship in the black-out in London, where they had a real black market going. This was kid's stuff for me.

So I took a washbag and started craftily buying a few biscuits and chocolates to flog to the geezers who ain't got nerve to go for themselves. But every now and then they'd make a raid in the barrack-room, stand to the beds, and they'd give the kitbag and everything a good going over. It was absolutely impossible to stuff any of this 'bent' gear under the bed.

The sergeant would come around for inspection every morning and drop a silver dollar on to the blankets. If that sack was not stretched drum-tight, and the coin failed to bounce, you were on the mat. So the slightest bend would give the game away. You couldn't smuggle a fag paper under it. But I somehow managed to craftily stuff the bits of gear—like it was gold or something!—out of sight, and never got caught.

I found the best way to get bits of stock for my little black-market racket was to creep to the area where they held an outdoor movie. There was a stall handy that sold tasty chocolate, chewing gum, and all that gear. But to do this little bit of villainy me and my mates—don't worry, I soon had guys grafting for me—had to sneak between the various patrols around the camp.

The Marines loved a reason for forming a guard patrol. They bunged a few rookies guard-sticks and they walked around areas guarding nothing from nothing. Some of these rookies used to suddenly become big, brave soldiers getting some sort of authority. One of my mates got himself a right crack across the head from a guy who was a bit handy at using the stick.

It was like a cops-and-robbers film, with me ducking and diving to get some Pogey Bait. Gawd knows what I would have done if something really worth while was going.

Kit-stealing was a real bother because it was impossible to pass what we called a 'Special' if you couldn't account for every bit of gear. With all those Marines locked up for so long, it was nothing to see a fair ole punch-up over a stolen pair of socks. Guys would be going around battling and cracking each other with sticks. It couldn't have been much worse in real action. At least you knew who the hell you were fighting against.

Every two minutes it seemed they were ordering a field day, with equipment being shined and beds made-up like new pins. Whenever any Marine with any sort of authority, even a one-striper, came into the hut the first guy who spotted him yelled 'Stand to sacks' and we all belted around the beds while he paraded around like some general.

I remember being out scraping up some Pogey Bait and hearing the call from our hut. 'Where's that goddamn Limey?' I heard this pumped-up private saying. I scampered in smartly, informing the tin god that I'd been patrolling the area like a good Marine should.

He made us line-up in three rows and then he informed the mob that some son-of-a-bitch had been pilfering Pogey Bait. 'I'm gonna stop your privileges, no movies for this platoon,' he said. All the guys in the hut who have been buying the bits of gear from me were staring daggers. I knew when this geezer finished his chat I was in for a sure belting from the boys.

Maybe the geezer tumbled I was the culprit, because he says, 'I suppose this Limey so-and-so has been balling things up again,' and I'm standing to attention, refusing to budge an eyelid. I've got my hat tipped down in regulation style to keep the head held high.

'I gotta feeling it was you, Downes, you wise guy,' he's saying, edging closer to me. Suddenly he pulls my hat right down over the eyes. I'm standing stiff but now weighing it up that I'm bound to get a whack in the belly from his stick. But before I could tense the muscles he belts me clean on the nose with a right-hander. The force of the blow knocked me clean through the three ranks. No blood was shed and, luckily, the old hooter stood up to the test well.

Getting that punch, and I swear it trembled every bone in my body, at least saved me from a going-over by the rest. They didn't approve of anyone, except themselves, doing the punching. It was no use crying to authority. You very likely finished up with an even bigger whacking.

But the black market went on and I was nifty enough never to have been nabbed.

The only things that really scared me were snakes. The camp training area was alive with them. When we were out on a mock battle and a sergeant would yell 'Hit the dirt' I was usually the last Marine to dive down. They were always on to me about this lateness obeying the order, but while diving didn't come naturally I was also having a good look around to make sure I wasn't falling on a snake. Long marches and general soldiering, driving an amphibious truck, it all came enjoyable to me. I liked the idea of building up strength and stamina. It wasn't the soldiering that bothered me—it was just the bull.

Somehow I survived this boot-training period, began learning a move or two, and they gave me the first leave. Going back to civilization was a great thought.

But I couldn't go through with the idea of marching down our Baltimore street in Marine uniform, with eyes at the windows and my family saying 'Here comes our "Tel the Marine" '. I choked them all changing into a civvy suit and getting a taxi home. Maybe I'd have stuck out the chest if I'd had just one stripe, or something, but since you can't get lower than the lowest private I ducked out.

From Baltimore I got my first stroke of luck, being posted to Quantico Camp, which was about eighty miles away. Now this was the way I figured out life in Marines was going to be. Driving back to the camp like Eisenhower was the way I liked it. I was eighteen and began to feel Mr. Big.

D

After the usual report-here, report-there lark, I boldly enquired who was coach of the boxing squad. Imagine how I felt when the guy tells me that since the boxing major had been posted there ain't no boxing squad. Well, whenever they are not certain what to do with a Marine they assign him on mess-duty. So I'm messing about, as they say, for about six weeks, dish-washing and what-not.

After this fill-in job they bung me in the Schools Demonstration Squad because Quantico is basically an officer-training camp and we're given the job of showing the cadets from colleges how to become Marines.

Quantico represents to the cadet officers what Paris Island was to boot Marines. So everyone gives these cadets hell because they know they are going to be officers—second Johns—and they're going to give *them* hell. Of course, if they really used their loaf they'd have been kinder to these clever guys, which might have made them friendlier as officers. But this system made sure the cadet had been given such a diabolical tough training he couldn't wait to take it out on somebody else. It was a vicious circle.

Mind you, I joined in the fun of having a go at them. My company was driving Amtrack trucks, which we drove off landing barges for beach assaults and had to drop the training troops off at the edge of the water. You can imagine how I used to pull the release lever and dump all the college boys into four feet of water!

I'd been serving about nine months without seeing a sign of boxing and just as I'm beginning to think this Marine game ain't no game I spot an advert in the camp paper to form a boxing team. At last I'm gonna get the gloves on. I get the C.O.'s permission to put my name up and I trooped down to the centre.

I thought half the Marine Corps had turned out to be in the boxing team. There must have been over 200 guys, all shapes and sizes, majority of them coloured, with flat noses, cauli-flower ears, and all inventing titles they held.

Half of them have only turned up to get the afternoon off from duties, and they've appointed a second John, straight out of college and as green as they grow 'em, to organize a squad of twenty boxers. With all the boys bumming their load about being champion of this and that he gets himself into a right state.

But within a day or two they've weeded out at least half because they didn't even know how to lace a pair of gloves. We got time off in the afternoons from normal duties to go training and road-running, which was something I loved. Then after a while we found our level. I was still among the last twenty. We were only a modest mob and when they took us around for inter-camp fights we usually won about three fights, with me, my old mate 'Country' Myers, and a Jewish heavy-weight called Len Kanthal. I thought this Kanthal geezer would have made himself bundles of cash when he became a pro. Good prospect he was.

When the Marines Corps championships came around I went through the prelims without too much bother and we were flown down to Miami, Florida—that's about 1,000 miles —for the Services final. I'm paired off with the Marine defending champion Randy Horne, who later became a world-rated pro welter-weight. We had a terrific battle—I won. As Horne was defending champion, it was a win that meant something.

'Country' and Kanthal got beat, so I was the only guy from our mob to win the Marine title. This made me King of the Castle. But the thing to remember about Services boxing is that few people recognize you out of the ring. Regulations demand that headguards are worn for all fights. It's a definite medical safety-measure, and while I reckoned headguards a right nuisance, I could understand why they were worn. But being masked did take a lot of the glamour out of the game.

So I was flattered in Miami when the local pro wizards, Chris and Angelo Dundee, who now handle a crack stable of champions, promote, train Cassius Clay, etc., told the *Miami Herald* reporter that I was the boy most likely to make the grade. And the guy with the closest view—the referee—supported them. He was Willie Pastrano, then a handsome welter- or middle-weight, who later fought six times in Britain

and became world light-heavy-weight champion. And in
1964 I was matched with him for the world title!

So you see I was really among the big boys with those three-
round Service battles. Randy Horne, a hell of a good fighter,
afterwards stayed on our Quantico team. I moved up a weight.
We also had Phil Ortiz, Richie Hill, and Charlie Newsome,
who even at that time could have handled themselves with the
pro's.

We rarely got pampered with home-crowd encouragement
and the experience I got with the Marines was, to a great
extent, responsible for the quick rise when I turned pro. I
beat Willie Hunter at Lee Field; Nick LaRosa at Quantico;
k.o.'d George Vinzant at Little Creek; regular wins at Michigan
State College.

At Miami Air Base—I stopped Larry Wright—I recall
Jake LaMotta, former world middle-weight champion, as
referee. Having guys like Pastrano and LaMotta officiating
helped lift the performance. I fought in Florida often and won
the State American Athletic Union title at the residential
Coral Gables Youth Centre in Miami, beating Reggie Perez
to win the outstanding-fighter trophy.

I always took good stock of the pro gyms in every town I
visited. People expect American gyms to be plush and perfectly
equipped. Fact is, a gym is a gym and most of them are just
grubby, smelly workshops where the real workmen practise.
I used to hang around the Fifth Street gym in Miami, where
Clay, Pastrano, and Luis Rodriguez trained to win world
titles. I liked being around the liniment and looking at good
fighters. You can't learn watching a load of rubbish working
out.

Anyway, having won the all-Marine title I was left alone
in Miami because they shipped out the losers from my squad.
They moved the winners on for training to Porky Gaults's
open-air camp. It was perfect, with marvellous weather, two
full-sized rings pitched in a field, and the conditions that
produce confidence.

The manager was Frank Veith, a good coach, and his ideas
contributed to later successes. I was very grateful for it. I

had already made up my mind that American coaches knew so much more, or at least had more idea on how to impart knowledge, than British instructors. My feelings for the standard of British trainers is pretty low. I won't be popular for saying it, but I've travelled enough to judge. Some of them shouldn't even hold a licence.

Perhaps being without any Quantico mates in Miami and changing the pattern could have upset my rhythm. I won about six in a row with stoppages and when the Marine team was shipped off to Oakland, California, right across from East to West Coast, I felt strange entering the All-Services championships. Yet I still had confidence, but I probably met a better-class or more experienced fighter, Larry Barrett, and recall losing for the first time in the Marines. Barrett was as tall as a beanpole.

Losing never bothered me, provided I'd fought well and picked up some experience. Quantico Camp had boxed against Michigan State for some years and it was always a cup-final match. One of the most satisfying wins I had was against Herb Odom, a coloured fellah, who was an idol at the college and had not been beaten. The local papers played up our match and we pulled in a big crowd. I got a big hand winning that one.

Michigan had produced some top-notch pro's, including Chuck Spieser, Chuck Davey, and Spider Webb, whom I fought later at Wembley. But that's another bloody story.

I had a bash, too, against Wisconsin College.

Frank Veith, who was a veteran master-sergeant from Pacific battles, always kept us working hard. This training fashioned the way I work now. Some say I might over-train, but I never worked half-hearted in the Marines and I can't stop now. We spent practically eight months of the year, a lot of it out of uniform, living in the Jock Strap section of the barracks and doing nothing but box. It was the greatest thing that ever happened to me.

In 1956 they entered our squad for the Golden Gloves. I managed to clout out the scrubbers drawn in the preliminaries, but you get up against some tidy fighters at the top.

At Fort Myer I was drawn against Rudy Sawyer, of the Navy Destroyer Force. I studied form—and still do—and found out that Sawyer had fought 118 times and lost only sixteen. I'd had fifty-six fights. He was a cracking coloured fighter. If you don't believe me just glance back at the high world ratings they gave Rudy when he turned pro.

I had no plan to run away from him, but I got some advice on how to do it from Lieutenant Wes Santee, who was with our mob and became America's best miler. In 1956 Santee had clocked 4 min. 0·5 sec. for the mile. Lieutenant-General Peacock, commandant at Quantico, called for me and explained how important it was to whip Sawyer. That's the kind of encouragement you get from the top in Marines. And you can't beat it. It was Sawyer's buddy, the lanky welter Barrett, who had licked me in the All-Service final the previous year, so the chips were really down.

But as much with hope as judgement I stormed into Sawyer, who did things those days that marked him a real pro. He kept stabbing out a left to steal points and I managed to time his lead just nicely to shoot a right-hand counter over the top in the second round. It caught Sawyer flush on the whiskers and floored him. It was only the second time he'd been down in his career. And he didn't arf look nice laying down.

Sawyer had a general cheering for him, too, so he had to get up. But he took the nine-count. I wasn't a big hitter. Who did I ever really knock out who knew how to fight? I just kept slinging plenty of punches to sicken 'em. Sawyer and me really had a terrific slug. We had the crowd standing on their chairs and when they collected the judges' papers I remember thinking that maybe he'd get the decision because it was close and he had the reputation. That counts.

But I also knew the knockdown was entitled to sway the vote in my favour—and it did. Defeating Rudy Sawyer was a bit of a feat. A reporter, Dick Slay, wrote: 'Only mad dogs and Englishmen go out in the noonday sun, says the ditty, and only Terry Downes, the transplanted Englishman, could end the string of Rudy Sawyer's sixteen consecutive victories in the Golden Gloves. Downes, baby-faced darling of the fans, and

Sawyer, pick of the experts, staged one of the most rousing battles . . .' Get a load of that baby-face bit.

They wrapped the scarlet-and-gold robe around me and two team-mates carried me out of the ring shoulder-high. Another reporter, in the *Washington Star*, wrote: 'The dead-game welter, Downes, mixing aggressiveness with beautiful boxing brought the house down with his performance.' And I loved every minute of it.

There was an even bigger build-up for the final when I had to fight George McCormack, a southpaw from Andrew's Air Base, whose commander, Brigadier-General Stoyte Ross, had ordered a ringside seat to cheer him on.

I hated southpaws—and still do. They fight like crabs. I didn't realize at the time that another southpaw called McCormack—John from Scotland—was going to steal the British middle-weight title away from me at Wembley. The first McCormack was tailor-made for my style. I waded in and walloped him out in 1 min. 52 sec. They gave me the Veteran of Foreign Wars trophy for this little tune-up. It was a great honour. It brought my run to nine wins on the trot.

Between times I reported back for normal Marine duties, and you can imagine how the other guys used to mix it for me with the sergeants. 'He's been away sunning himself while we've done the work,' they'd be saying. So I got rounded up for just about every guard or duty that was going. I became the platoon's automatic volunteer. 'Did you put your hand up?' they'd say. 'No, sir,' I'd reply. 'You should have done. You'll do,' was a stock finish.

The 1956 Inter-Services championships brought out a real crack lot. Quantico and credit coach Veith got four Marine champions, and I was lucky enough to get the 'Outstanding Boxer' award again, beating the Pacific champion Bob Griffin in the Marine Corps finals at Camp Lejeune. The Army, Navy, and Air Force paraded their entrants for the Service punch-up and I scored a big hit, beating Pearce Lane, later chosen to represent the U.S. at the Melbourne Olympics.

When we posed with the winning trophies I realized what a useful mob I'd joined. Luis Molina, now a world-rated pro light-weight, was the light-weight winner; Randy Horne was there again as light-welter king; Jim Boyd, a big-name pro cruiser; Jose Torres, world-rated as a middle after teaming up with Cus D'Amato, and Pete Rademacher, Olympic champion whose first pro fight was with Floyd Patterson for the world title, were the other winners.

To win the qualifying Marine championship I had to win a fight each night for four nights. This was better than pro practice. Having stuck out most of the top boys I was nominated to compete in the Olympic trials. A big deal.

Seven Marines went to Albany, New York, where 100 fighters were punching it out for the East Coast trials. I was the only Marine to survive the stint. I fought four times in twenty-four hours. I had no trouble stopping Gordon Beauchamp in one round. But the next guy, Bill Pickett, from the New York Police Athletic League, was tough and knew the business. Evidence? Seven years later he came to Manchester and outpointed Harry Scott in a TV fight.

But Pickett wasn't exactly the nippy kid I'd remembered. He was still cute enough to beat Scott, but, according to a smart 'exposé' by the Daily Mail, Pickett had not been officially discharged from an after-care clinic in Rockland State Hospital where he'd been committed as an alcoholic by the Supreme Court of New York in 1962 and stayed a year.

To top it up, Pickett, staying in England for a second fight, was fined £150 in Salford, where he pleaded guilty to charges of indecently assaulting and causing bodily harm to the twelve-year-old daughter of the owner of a Salford hotel.

The local Magistrate said, 'In the ordinary way it may well have been that you ought to have gone to prison. . . .' His defending lawyer said in court, 'The public of this country would well be rid of him at an early date.' Pickett was packed off home within twenty-four hours.

It was a diabolical fade-out for a guy I thought looked a good fighter. Where was his guidance? This case brought a stricter control on the admittance of American fighters to Britain and they can't come in unaccompanied.

The final ticket to the National Olympic trials was to beat

Bob Rigolosi, of Syracuse. I did it easily. The Baltimore report read: 'Other team coaches and old boxing hands were quick to notice Terry Downes's ring ability and lent their verbal support and advice.'

Just to give a line on the class of these trials I talked in the dressing-room to a coupla coloured boys who both won and afterwards became world-rated pros. They were light-heavy Doug Jones and heavy Alonzo Johnson.

Then somebody checked up on the qualifications and tumbled I was English. I needed another year in the States before I could become eligible for citizenship. Newspapers campaigned for me, but three-year Service qualification didn't count. I was out. I hadn't minded losing in a Golden Gloves event because even Rocky Marciano failed that one. But being turned down for Melbourne was a real choker. When the final trials were decided I'd beaten three of the four finalists—including, of course, Pearce Lane.

Luckily, my Service time was running out and I was able to think about my future to take my mind off the disappointment. But service in the Leathernecks had built up an amateur reputation, given me strength and confidence, a chance to move in the men's world, and some great coaching. It was definitely the finest thing that could have happened to me.

ROUND 4

I Turn Pro

I FOUGHT fifty-one times as a Marine and had never been off my feet. When you consider I was knocking around in the class of Randy Horne, Rudy Sawyer, Doug Jones, Pete Rademacher, Jose Torres—a league a lot tougher than the juniors I'd left in London—it was a pretty good record. All told, I'd chalked-up about eighty-five bouts and lost five over a period of five years.

All this time I'd kept close watch on the pro game, following the rise and fall of fighters, checking up on managers. The one thing for certain I learned was to be in good hands if I turned pro. I didn't want a manager I could take home to tea but a man who knew the angles and had the right connections. I didn't want some likable guy who hadn't been around and would learn his business on me. I had to get me a man who was 'in'.

Down at the Baltimore Y.M.C.A. we had a very enthusiastic helper, Lou Leavey, who used to father the fighters and run us around in his car. You get these fellahs who like to be around with boxers and encourage them in all stages of the game. Some are just a bunch of gymnasium lawyers who talk a lot of nonsense and, sometimes, influence fighters; others offer genuine help. Leavey was a bit of both.

My Service time was running out and I was more or less laying about looking for the right connections to become a pro. I figured a little bit of something was better than a lot of nothing, so I was determined to wait until Mr. Right arrived. Dad, a shrewd nut, was also weighing-up the situation. Eventually, on the advice of John Seagroves, a *Baltimore Sun*

62

reporter, Leavey agreed to take us to New York and meet Irving Cohen, whom I knew had handled Rocky Graziano (the character ex-world champion), Billy Graham (puncher, not preacher), and Walter Cartier. We met at the Edison Hotel off Broadway at Times Square, which was a favourite hang-out for the fight mob.

I obviously didn't know the full strength about management, so when Cohen, a dapper man and slick talker, explained that he couldn't handle me but he'd keep an eye on things if I signed with Walter Cartier it seemed O.K. to me. With Cartier was his lawyer brother Vincent. You just don't ask too many questions about such things in the American fight game. If Cohen thought this was a good idea it must have been a good idea. I had to be impressed with a guy who'd managed Graziano. Later when I read Graziano's lifestory he made it obvious that Cohen had plenty of 'help'.

Lou Leavey was no mug, though, because he declared himself in the action and agreed to have a piece of my contract. I was under-aged and later they sent contracts for Dad, as guardian, to sign. Neither of us knew at the time that neither Leavey nor Cartier were licensed managers. So the deal wasn't legal.

One of the sweeteners attached to this deal was $500 (£178), which Dad explained was wanted to pay fares and maybe some expenses for a trip to London. We had agreed to stay in Baltimore, but Dad and I fancied a visit home to see the relations before I got down to professional fighting.

Mum and Sylvie stayed in Baltimore while we hopped over to England. One of the first things I did was to call and say 'Thanks' to Tim Riley, editor of *Boxing News*—the trade paper in Britain—who had given me some encouraging write-ups while I was in the Marines. I liked moving around Fleet Street. I knew the value of publicity, and any fighter who says he doesn't enjoy reading his name in print is a liar and has no right in the business.

In September 1956 *Boxing News* had given me a full-page plug after winning the American Olympic trial. Reg Gutteridge, of the *London Evening News*, also gave me a favourable mention in his amateur column. They were the first home writers to give me publicity. I want especially to thank them. Eight years later they are still among my friends—and sternest critics.

While I was just killing time in London I couldn't resist keeping in trim, but because of the part-promises I'd made to Cartier and Leavey I steered clear of pro gyms in London. So, at Tim Riley's suggestion, I enrolled at Fisher amateur club in Bermondsey, which was a bit of a drag from Paddington but had a good team. They rigged me out in the black vest with white hoop and tried to provide me with sparring-partners. I must admit I thought the difference between these club kids and the tough Americans I'd been used to fighting was a bit amusing.

They'd stand all stiff and upright, sometimes stamping their front foot as they punched. They seemed real amateurs compared with the hard nuts I'd been meeting in the Marines. Because I couldn't get worthwhile sparring I actually had to *pay* to bring a pro partner into a gym!

Harry Carpenter, then a columnist with the *Daily Mail*, sorted me out to write a column. I was flattered. What did I mean in England? I posed for a photo with my uncle Bill's twenty-one-year-old taxi and after the interview the headline read: 'Terry toppled Yanks, now he can show us.' Right away I got the reputation of being a big-head.

I'd told the writer that the fighters I'd seen here couldn't hold a candle to the Yanks. I told him that there were coloured preliminary fighters in the States who could whip British champions. I told him that in three weeks in London I'd only managed ten rounds' sparring practice. In the States I could have got that in two nights. I was also shocked to sit in a gym and watch boys working out without even sparring. I could see this hit-and-hop-it style was not for me. British boxing just wasn't rough enough.

Well, you can imagine that I was unpopular for this opinion. But I said all those things because I honestly believed them to be true. I wasn't intending to sound like a big-head, and certainly not to belittle anyone. It was just a sincere opinion.

Coventry. He'd beaten Dick Tiger, who later became world middle-weight champion—besides beating me.

This Lynas hadn't been stopped (he'd fought Tiger twice) and seemed a bit of a hard nut. It didn't make any impression on me that he hadn't been stopped. There could always be a first time. So I did the old flashy jig into the ring again, got the usual 'bird', and was weighing-up Lynas while the referee, Tommy Little, was giving a few words of instruction before the off.

I steamed in and landed a lot of punches, but it didn't make the slightest impression. I thought to myself, 'Blimey, Tel, you've got a right hard one here,' and noticed he led with his face a bit. That could have been his own bluff to stop me hitting him up the belly. If I hadn't switched to the body in the second round I think I'd still be cracking away now at his chin without moving him.

A left hook downstairs stopped Lynas in his tracks. He'd suddenly changed. So I clobbered him fast around the head and he went down for eight. The bell rang before I could really get weaving again, but I went out in the third and picked off a dozen different punches that bewildered him. A left hook sent him slithering sideways down and, though he was as game as a bigel climbing up at nine, the referee caught him in his arms—and I'd won. Looking back I honestly can't list the first two fights as pushovers, though I'd won them easily enough. Longo and Lynas were not 'over-the-top' fighters. That's why I felt so encouraged to have licked them.

The editor of *Boxing News* gave me a terrific, embarrassing write-up, headed 'Downes was Dynamite', and said:

'Whisper it amongst yourselves, not too loudly—just yet, but Britain has found another crashing, bashing, dashing Kid; yes, another Ted Kid Lewis. Downes is the name, or Terry the Terrible. Headlining Jack Solomons' annual charity promotion at Manor Place Baths, Downes simply demolished Jimmy Lynas inside three rounds and Lynas hasn't had that happen to him before in almost five years of fighting.

'Downes' performance was on a par to the early fights of Randy Turpin. No British middle has shown such ferocity, urge to win in the quickest possible time, or tireless aggression, for years. Downes hasn't got Turpin's classic punches, he doesn't wait for an opening like Turpin used to do, but he sets about his task with the same speed, the same murderous intent, and like Turpin will quickly become great box-office.

'Like the great Lewis, Downes smothers his opponents from all angles. He doesn't give a fig for the other man's intentions, or punches. Aggression and yet more aggression. To hell with anything but quick victory, that's Terry's motto, and British rings have been crying out for a fighter like it for years.'

Peter Wilson, who does not normally bother to report local-hall stuff, wrote another flattering column. Peter had his digs at me in his time, but he gave me a big start and fair do's when I deserved it. His story was headed 'The Real Mean Fighter'. He said I'd again stolen the show, and wrote: 'Frankly, I do not know any British-born middle on whom I would wager much money to stay the championship distance with Downes.'

This was big praise after my second fight from a writer who'd probably covered more fights around the world than anyone else. He'd seen the greatest. Can you wonder that I was a bit bouncy?

The *Daily Herald* headlined: 'Whiz Kid Downes wins with Perfect Punch.'

The Star writer said: 'I can see Terry Downes becoming a big problem to the Boxing Board of Control. Such a problem, in fact, that I shall not be surprised if he decides to go back to America . . . another explosive victory and there will be few middle-weights for the Board to consider as reasonable opponents for Downes.'

You won't believe it, but one writer actually reckoned I'd be ready for Sugar Ray Robinson within a year! Little did I know it, but the big fall was about to come. Only six days after my twenty-first birthday—and I didn't take any time out to celebrate—I was matched at Shoreditch Town Hall against Dick Tiger, a Nigerian who worked in a paint factory in Liverpool and, to me, was just another trial horse. Later they told me his real name was Richard Ihetu, with his own family 'tribe' in Lagos. After the fight I-hated-HIM.

He had had eleven fights in England, lost the first four, and then his ninth fight. Lynas had won and lost against him, so the form looked O.K. Two weeks before he boxed me, Tiger turned in a good performance stopping Johnny Read at the National Sporting Club in two, and having Johnny up and down more times than I care to count. But as Johnny was emigrating to Canada I figured he wasn't too worried about being game that night.

At the weigh-in I could see Tiger was a well-built fighter, but was surprised when he came in three pounds over-weight. We were matched at 11 st. 8 lb. He had an hour to make some attempt to get weight off, though I knew he'd never make it. But after he'd had a little skip I was satisfied and the official weights were me at 11 st. 3½ lb. and Tiger one ounce inside 11 st. 9 lb. He wasn't exactly a pushover for me to give that kind of weight away.

But the shrewd punters were betting 5—1 against Tiger, which on paper made it no match. Yet how many smart alecs were afterwards saying that it was a bad match for me? I never heard anyone saying it before the fight.

Shoreditch Town Hall is a smoky, compact little arena, with the balcony boys practically breathing down your neck. It's a tremendous atmosphere. I doubt if I've ever seen a hall where the crowd can succeed in getting the fighters 'at it'. The crowd help to make good fights. Tiger and me didn't need any encouragment—though we got it.

My ring entrance, for the third time, was being a bit more accepted, though the wags still had a go. The seats closest to the ring were not only packed with pressmen but had the people in the trade there. Solomons again came to see me fight. Astaire, by the way, was seated opposite the ring, facing my corner. He was always more excited than me.

Astaire has never been in a corner and says it's better to employ more qualified seconds so he can watch the fight with more detachment. Sometimes he sees more from outside and can send a message to the cornermen. From what I've seen of some managers they are a bigger handicap than help to their fighters in the corner. At least Astaire was smart enough to stay out. Some guys I could name ought to be arrested for incompetence.

As usual, I wasn't treating an opponent too lightly. I'd trained as hard as I knew, but thought Tiger couldn't be too great, because I was matched again, at Streatham, a week later. Getting £125 for only a third fight was good pay. I think Tiger got about £60. A few years later they couldn't get us together for £30,000!

The crowd that went wild with excitement at Shoreditch didn't know they were watching two future world middle-weight champions—especially the way I finished up. I sailed into Tiger right from the bell, but he tagged me with a peach of a left hook—I can still feel the punch!—and the next thing I knew he was looking a much bigger middle-weight than me. That's because I was on the floor looking up at him.

Only having ever taken one count in my life—against Mickey Rosette in Atlantic City—I wasn't experienced enough to start looking for help from the corner. (The only real help they can give is sympathetic.) Thinking in my daze that the count would go on to a compulsory eight, as they did in the States, I got up at three. I felt a right berk being on the floor, anyway. Me, the Whiz Kid, next world champion, killer, and all that jazz, laying about on the deck against a geezer nobody reckoned. I mean, you just have to get up quick.

But before I could dust my gloves off or consider what I'd have to do next the ref calls 'Box on' and I was choked enough to wish I'd gone down again. That taught me not to get busy and get up too early. I was catching on.

But my legs were feeling a bit dodgy, and the crowd faces were still a bit out of focus when Tiger belted into me again. Another punch—I didn't bother to stop to ask what kind it was —stuck me on the deck again. That resin wasn't 'arf dirtying my nice scarlet shorts. This time I waited until the ref called 'seven' before I stirred. I was hurt but had no intention of staying down. I thought I'd got myself a right one here, so the only thing to do is start belting back.

We were slashing away like good 'uns when the first bell rang. To me it sounded like an orchestra. I could see by the

faces of my seconds that I'd taken some stick. They looked more
worried than me. My feeling was not so much of hurt but of
wounded pride. While the seconds were rabbiting—talking—
in my ear I was considering what I'd have to do to hold this
Tiger. He sat in the other corner like an ebony statue, all
muscles and strength.

I stormed out for the second, not really refreshed but trying
to kid Tiger that I'd recovered. He wasn't impressed. The
next thing I know he's taken another liberty and knocked me
down again. 'What's going on here?' I was saying to myself
as the crowd were going mad, some of them banging on the
ring apron to make me get up.

I don't know why they worried—I never even considered
staying down. I was getting the dead needle.

I gritted my teeth and nearly bit through the gumshield
when I got up at 'eight'—and it was the last time I fancied
being down. I steamed into Tiger, throwing everything I'd
got, and I'm pleased to say he was warned for laying-on and
butting—which our refs so politely call 'careless use of the head'.
But Tiger could take a good whack.

The first two rounds had sapped a bit of strength from me and
it takes a few rounds to get over it. But I began whacking Tiger
around the body, and thumped him under the heart enough
to start taking the play away from him. At least I'd started
pulling the points back. But what a terrific battle it was. The
crowd were going mad—and so were the big mob who couldn't
get into the hall.

But my right eye was swollen, and in the sixth I was cut
pretty badly over the left eye, near the bridge of the nose.
When I got back to the corner Snowy and the other seconds
reckoned the injuries bad enough for me to retire. I was willing
to fight on, but if they can't patch the cut I'm wasting my time.
They surrendered for me. I was choked.

I made a few cracks in the dressing-room when the reporters
asked who I'd fight next. 'The geezer who just made that
match,' I told them. I also said I'd have to start all over again
—with the fly-weights.

I mean, it was no use me moaning and you've got to say

F

something if only to put on a front. The Press were pretty fair to me and I was pleased. The *Daily Telegraph* said: 'Downes gets Glory in Defeat', and Lainson Wood (what a great character he was! He could fall asleep during a fight, or even a training session, and write a great story just the same) said: 'Downes came out of the defeat with reputation enriched after six rounds of terrific punching and some clever manœuvring . . . he has established himself as a money-spinner and his future seems assured.'

Frank McGhee, in the *Daily Mirror*, wrote: 'Another British hope has crashed into the dust of disappointment', and described the last round with ' . . . more bad luck in store for Downes. Right at the end of the round, after a mid-ring clash of heads for which Tiger was warned, the Paddington boy came out with a bruise the size of a pigeon's egg under his right eye.'

Tommy Farr, the old heavy-weight champion, said in his *Sunday Pictorial* column: 'British boxing has a twenty-two-carat prospect in Terry Downes,' and then advised me to consider more defence. I listened.

Gilbert Odd, another experienced writer, said: 'Strangely enough, had the fight gone the distance Terry might have got the referee's nod.' That might convince those who since have said that I was never in with a chance.

Commercially, I'd been a big hit because this was the first show staged without the heavy entertainment tax that had been crippling boxing. The show had completely sold out.

I never had the needle with anyone about the match except myself for holding my hands too low at the start. To me it was just an ordinary fight and at the time I couldn't see a bad match being made for me. That's how I felt.

I thought I could have easily have won as lost. Barring the cuts and getting knocked over in the first, I fancied I would have swarmed all over Tiger before the end because at the time I reckoned to be in better condition. A mug in a street fight is liable to knock you over if you let him, so I wasn't really upset. It was some consolation later, of course, when I knew I'd lost to a good man when Tiger won the Empire title and then whipped Gene Fullmer for the world title.

Yet I still felt a lot of critics over-rated Tiger even at his best. He was a good, strong fighter who took a lot of beating. But he's predictable. That's why I figured Joey Giardello, a smart operator, would have learned enough from their first two fights to take the title from Tiger. One newspaper wrote this opinion from me before the fight—so you'll know I'm not bluffing.

A lot of writers—some are inclined to follow a leader—said I should stay away from Tiger. I ain't saying I was ever in a real hurry to fight him, but for the right kind of money, under the right conditions, I'd have loved to meet him again. Honest, I figured I could beat him. But boxing politics kept us apart.

We did try to make offers, but Tiger was pumped-up to make replies like, 'Let Downes win the British title first'. After I had vacated the British title I still think Tiger was a right mug and wrongly advised not to have cashed-in fighting me—we'd have drawn a bomb of money—instead of blowing his title for comparative chicken-feed to Giardello, who was probably picked as a soft touch.

One thing was certain after the Tiger fight—I had to hold an inquest. How comes I lost? I wasn't satisfied with the way things were going at the gym. I felt I wasn't being taught enough. Snowy was doing his job the way he figured was best, but it didn't suit me. All boxers need encouraging and I felt Snowy was neglecting me. Maybe that was his way of working.

If I was reckoned impetuous in the ring, I was also just as impetuous buying an engagement-ring. Me and Barbara were going that steady. On the way back from the Tiger fight—she cried all the way through it—she's crying again in the car and saying, 'Look at your face,' but I figured she's got to get used to it. Fighting was my life and a few tears for two minutes weren't going to alter all the years I'd spent training and working to an ambition.

I was a professional fighter—so let her cry. All the punches I'd taken and *she* was crying. I was the one who could have cried. But defeat didn't bother me. It was the way I fought that always concerned me. Cuts meant absolutely nothing to me. I suppose that sounds soppy, but if you're a professional

fighter you've got to expect and accept cuts like some occupational hazard.

But you'd be surprised how many people came up to me and
said fighters never get over a beating like the one I got. (Like
Tiger hadn't even taken a punch!) I'd never be the same, they
said. I sometimes think boxing is full of know-nothings. I
wonder how they felt when I won the world title four years
later!

O.K., so a beating can't help, but a young guy, trained and
determined, can get over one hard punch-up. Less than a
month after the Tiger fight I insisted on fighting again. So I
was back at Harringay on Solomons' annual Derby Eve show
against Alan Dean, from the North of England, who had
beaten Tiger, so he was just the type of rival they wanted.
Everyone was telling Dean how to beat Downes. Even the
newspaper boys became trainers by writing how to whip me.
Just go straight in and bang away, they said. This encouraged
Dean to go winging in and because he threw so many punches,
naturally he landed with some. But they were all soppy
punches and I kept a bit restrained and let him burn himself
out a bit. Gave him his head.

Dean did all his fighting in the first and when it didn't
make much difference to me he started blowing-up a bit.
From then on he just soaked up my punches. I'd slowed down
to get a bit more power in them. I took the fight with a breeze,
and by the fourth the referee, and certainly Dean, had had
enough. The fight was stopped, though I don't remember
Dean being off his feet. But he was banged-up pretty good.

For the first time I actually had a weight advantage of $1\frac{1}{2}$ lb.
I began adding a bit of weight with all the build-up work I'd
done. I went in at 11 st. 6 lb., the middle limit.

Just two weeks later I was fighting again. No messing about
with me or my manager. I thrived on work. And the match-
makers were almost lining up to get me. Like or dislike,
whether they thought I could fight or not, I gave value. I
can't stand frauds who go into a ring looking to duck and dive
and hope to survive without hardly getting hit. It ain't smart
getting hit too much, I know, but a fighter should also be an

entertainer. If a fighter fancies running he should take up athletics.

At Streatham Ice Rink on June 18 I was paired off with Sammy Hamilton, of Belfast, whose record suggested he'd give me a good go. The only time Hamilton had been halted was with a cut mouth. Otherwise he was the type to stay the course.

I went in banging away, as usual, because my style demands that I saturate the other guy with punches enough for him to either quit or go down. I don't usually reckon to stop anyone with one punch. When Hamilton shot a right-hander at me, and landed, there was a big cheer, so it gives you an idea of the crowd's reaction. They always rooted for someone to stop me. The English seem to plead for a successful fighter, yet when a promising one comes along people still enjoy seeing him licked. That even goes for the fight fraternity—and they should know better.

But the cheer, of course, didn't bother me none, but just made me work harder. Coming out for the third I winked at Hamilton as if to acknowledge that I was enjoying the fight. I was. I always respect a man who has a go. But I was also thinking this was going to be Sammy's last round. It was. I banged away fast to the body and before he could collapse the ref called me off.

These fights, of course, were still scheduled eight-rounders. I hadn't dropped in class and a referee had not been bothered with points, for or against, in my five fights. Against Hamilton I knocked-up my left hand and though I can't say it pained me much in the fight I felt it swelling in the dressing-room.

I was a bit surprised when Snowy Buckingham was putting his coat on and saying he'd see me in the gym the next week. Maybe I wanted fussing. But whatever it was I'd made up my mind, there and then, for a change. Usually fighters have to let managers call the tune for their entire career, if not certainly for the first dozen fights. But because I knew exactly what I expected from the fight-game I was a pretty demanding geezer from the start. Astaire understood me and always discussed my problems sensibly.

He gave me a lift home and I told him that I wasn't satisfied with Snowy. Maybe it was a clash of personalities. But I insisted on a change—and got it.

I was due to fight a Scot, John Woollard, at Shoreditch only seven days after the Streatham win. My hand was dodgy with fluid causing a swelling, but I wasn't going to miss another good earner. I'd got £150 for beating Hamilton and that's good pay for that kind of job.

Astaire introduced me to Tom Ryder, who lived near me at Paddington, and had trained at an amateur club and was doing a good job with Les Morgan whom Astaire handled. He seemed a rough-and-ready Cockney, and it was O.K. by me to become the trainer. He'd look me over and I'd weighed him up. We changed gyms to a basement off Warren Street, in Euston, where the car-dealers buy and sell. It was an old-established gaff, a bit of a dump I thought, but all right for the job. Some good fighters worked-out there.

Ryder was a bit of a taskmaster and made me work hard. But that's what I wanted. I couldn't work hard enough, so we got along fine. He had his ideas about making me box a bit more and fight a bit less. When I met Woollard I tried to brain-wash myself to do a bit of both. Ryder was trying to keep the reins on me. But I really have to convince myself that I must box. And when I tumbled Woollard, who was a tough enough fighter, wasn't buckling, I piled in. My hand had blown up again in the first, but I didn't mention it in the corner.

The fight was nearly as thrilling as the one in the same ring with Tiger. We really set about each other. In the fifth my ear began to bleed, my eyebrow was nicked, and I began to realize I was really in a tough business. Woollard was about to drop to the floor in the sixth when the bell rang, but the crowd were going so crazy that nobody heard it. The referee, a school sportsmaster, Bill Williams, had to ask the timekeeper to bang the gong harder.

I had him down for a quick count in the fifth, but in the seventh he went down again for eight. Woollard was a real game guy. He tried getting up, but his legs were rubbery and the referee stepped in. It was the longest distance I'd ever travelled, and I have a nice few souvenirs to remember it.

Because of the injuries and considering I'd had six good fights in two months, I was told to rest. I thought Astaire and Ryder were silly suggesting time off, because I was still raring to go. But they were right. I'd have burned up too easily.

From June 17 I waited until September 17 for a return to Harringay Arena and the best-purse fight so far. I was getting £225 in only my seventh fight against Lew Lazar, a Jewish boy from a well-known Aldgate family. He was a good boxer and different from the others I'd met. He was rated high. British boxers were still nothing but just names to me, so I went on the judgment of my manager. So long as I was taking a step-up with each fight I was satisfied.

My mum and dad were still in Baltimore and neither had seen me fight in England. I used to write maybe once a week if they were lucky, but always sent off some newspaper-cuttings to keep them informed. I was lodging with an aunt at Hallfield Estate in Paddington, going out early in the mornings for road-work around Hyde Park, and still humping those bales of cloth around in Shoreditch.

When I made a date with Barbara she accepted that I'd be home around 9.30. I couldn't fight after too many late nights. So Barbara never had the normal courtship. She understood what my career meant to me. I often wondered whether I really deserved her. But I was good to her. I began buying her better-priced seats to see me fight! She'd started in the back row and was coming forward bit by bit.

When I saw Lazar at the weighing-in I remembered Ryder's advice that though he was a good left-hand jabber he could be hit with left-hands. By the look of his face, with a nose banged about a bit, somebody had hit him. It's always been amazing to me when people start talking about how brilliant somebody boxed and when I see them they're marked-up pretty good. Yet a lot of the so-called rough fighters haven't a mark!

The critics always rave about Howard Winstone's scientific boxing—and I agree with them—but he's got a nice cauliflower ear to keep him company.

Lazar had appeared in the first fight to open commercial

TV in Britain. He'd also fought the champion, Pat McAteer, and was Southern Area champion. We had a great battle— and I won on points over eight rounds. *Boxing News* said: 'What a game fighter is Lew Lazar. After his fight with Terry Downes you could have conservatively estimated his chances of winning as one in a thousand. His chances of lasting the distance could have been no more than one in a hundred. Yet Lew was there at the finish, bloody, bruised, and badly battered.'

I had to be satisfied beating an experienced performer, but I wasn't really happy at having to settle for points. I'd put Lazar down *six* times. I should have finished him. But few could nail Lew. Not only was he a game customer but good and slippery with it. It was Lew's fifty-sixth pro fight to my seventh. He didn't lose another fight that year.

Two weeks later I was back in the ring again, at my insistence, and they dug up a welter-weight, Derek Liversidge, who came from the sticks, to meet me at Shoreditch. I was becoming a favourite there and a big draw. I tumbled that I was much better off boxing in England than in America as I'd intended. The crowds were responding marvellously, I was earning more than I was really entitled to, and even the war-dance which began as a bit of a joke was being accepted.

Liversidge was twenty and had lost only one of twenty-three fights. I had about 4 lb. advantage and I expected him to use the ring and poke out lefts. He did. And in the first round I was cut *over* the left eye for the first time. I knew I was in a bleeding business.

I switched to the reliable body-attacking, pumped a couple of good shots to the belly, and Liversidge crumbled up. He went down four times. It was all over in five minutes thirty seconds.

After the fight I started to become the best customer at Moorfields Eye Hospital, which is only a stone's throw from Shoreditch Town Hall. I don't believe in being stitched-up in a dressing-room, and went to hospital, where they get plenty of practice, and asked them to do a nice job. Considering they do it for free—except for the drink money I always bunged in the collection box—Moorfields did a marvellous job. It wasn't much of a cut, but I was taking no chances.

In the crowd at Shoreditch was Jimmy Carter, of America, who had been world light-weight champion. He was in town to fight Willie Toweel. I'd watched Carter a lot in the States and reckoned him a good workman, so I listened when he said I should shorten my stride and shorten the punches. I've always boxed with the legs spread a bit too far, but it's been hard to break the habit. I did it to get better punch leverage

The Shoreditch fight also brought me a new partner. Sam Burns, whom I'd seen around with Jarvis Astaire, became my deputy manager because Astaire was either out of the country or concerned somewhere with business. I knew Sam was a shrewd sort. His father Sid had been a top-class fighter in his day and gone the distance with Georges Carpentier. Sam had also worked with Jack Solomons for about twelve years, travelled around the world, and knew the business. He'd managed Eddie Thomas, a champion, and had Bobby Neill, who became champion. He was the kind of man I was glad to have around me.

Later in my career Astaire and Burns became my official co-managers. Jarvis explained that often he would be tied up in his expanding business affairs and Sam would be responsible for me, and I can't say enough about how well our partnership has worked. I had no idea at the time that Sam and I were going to share in big business.

Most fighters, I've found, are always having their arguments with managers. Some get to the stage where they'd sooner fight their managers for nothing than go into the ring. I've had the few words here and there with Jarvis and Sam, but I've always trusted them and been grateful for their friendship. I'd like to record my thanks to them in this book.

Having met Carter and Burns at Shoreditch, I also had a date with John Bull. I'd been called-up for National Service in the Army. Leave off, I thought, I must have done my whack in the Marines. Anyway . . . I was on parade the next day.

ROUND 6

Earning a few Quid

I HAD to enrol with the Army at Hounslow, so when my dad started bragging about his service I could always tell him I was an old soldier. Mind you, I'll bet T. R. Downes, Private, was one of the shortest-serving in history. I was discharged, with all the honours, after twenty-four hours!

No villainy, or working my ticket, but it was a token-day service because I'd done the full stint as a regular in America. A combined five years with the armies of both countries would have been a bit too strong for me.

Anyway, having got that little lark over with, I had to find somewhere else to live. Some busybody had written to the Paddington Borough Council telling them I was living with my aunt at the council-owned flats. Lodgers are banned—even though I was a legit relative. So I couldn't risk having the aunt turned out. My cousin Pat had taken over a car-lot and shop in Manor Road, Harlesden, and he said there was an old house nearby for sale. So Downesey moved into the property business.

I had to pay £2,000 for the house and from my fights I put down about £700 deposit. Being able to do this after eight fights proved to me that boxing was a good game. I was still working for a crust as well.

That's what turned me into a poor man's Charlie Clore with the take-over house. It was a deal I'd done without seeking advice. And it helped start me thinking about business besides boxing. Whatever happened, I knew I wouldn't end up broke. It was not much use having money in the bank unless you could make it work for you. So I speculated and made the money do the graft.

Meanwhile, I'd told Mum and Dad, still in the States, about courting Barbara and, because they hadn't seen her, they naturally felt I might be tying myself up and wrecking all the years I'd worked to be a fighter. You know what mums are. It's true that if a fighter or any athlete gets married to a wrong 'un his days are numbered.

So Mum and Dad sailed home and I took Barbara with me to meet them at Southampton. All was well and it's been plain sailing ever since.

One of the first callers we had in Manor Road was Mickey Duff, the matchmaker I first met in the gym, who worked at Shoreditch and Leyton, etc. Whenever he used to turn up I knew there was some business doing and used to be on my guard. Mickey is a better talker than I am a fighter.

He said he'd been trying to contact Sam Burns because his top-of-the-bill had let him down at Leyton Baths and would I jump in? I think the fight was due in three days. Anyway, I let him chat on, knowing that I'd take the fight if Sam okayed it, and he said he could sign Eddie Phillips, who came out of Leamington and had been a spar-mate to Randy Turpin. I think Phillips was living in Scotland at the time. Sparring with Turpin couldn't have helped his health, I thought, so he should be punched-out a bit.

Duff said he'd top-up the purse money if I did him a favour and took the fight. I'd have taken the fight for about £100, because that's all it was worth. He offered £200. So who's arguing?

As it turned out, I won the fight like just another outing. I trimmed down to 11 st. 3 lb., so I wasn't in a flabby shape for a substitute. I was always fit. To Phillips's credit, he took everything I aimed without going down and when the fight was finished in the third the referee was criticized both for stopping the fight too soon and for not stopping it earlier! The referee was Eddie Maguire, a South African who had been a top middle in Britain before the war.

'Downes was Devastating' said the headline in *Boxing News*. I just thought it was a good work-out.

I was back working in the warehouse when either Astaire

or Burns telephoned to tell me I'd been booked to fight Les Allen, of Bedworth, in a big charity show at Empress Hall, Earls Court, which is now demolished for a big government office block. I was getting £400! It seemed like a fortune to me and I had to tell somebody. I sorted out Ted, the geezer from the stockroom I grafted with. He reckoned the purse was handsome. I probably choked him, as a worker getting about a tenner a week, bragging about my big pay-day. He probably thought I was a nice sort of geezer giving him aggravation. He couldn't have cared less.

But this jump into the big-time so pleased me I fancied giving up work. I chatted it over with Benny Schmidt, and explained that it was a fair way to travel to work and I wanted to give more time to my training. He understood.

But going into the Allen fight I made a shocking ricket. Me and Barbara had been visiting several of my relations on the Sunday prior to the Tuesday fight. I suppose I swagged too many cups of tea and cakes, because when I checked the weight in the gym, twenty-four hours before the fight, I'd blown-up to 11 st. 10 lb.—the highest I'd ever scaled.

Ryder, rightly, gave me a right rollicking and I had to work-out a bit harder than we planned. I sweated off about 2 lb. and Tom gave me orders to dry-out overnight and I'd be just the right weight at the one o'clock weigh-in. I was so nervous I never touched any liquids. I was parched. Not ever having had weight troubles, I wasn't sure how to control my weight. I'd obviously gone too strong drying-out and was shocked when I came in at 11 st. 4½ lb. Shifting about 6 lb. overnight was ridiculous. But it was my fault.

Allen was a cagey and experienced fighter who knew the ropes and had been in with the best. For the first time in my life I really felt tired in a fight. Whenever I charged in Allen would tie me up in knots. He really knew the game. The last thing in the world he wanted was to let me work away with both hands. So he did a good job messing me about.

I went back to the corner after about five rounds really whacked out. It was the first time I'd asked seconds to rub my arms and legs. But I wasn't making any big show about being

With Paul Pender again, winning the world title at Wembley, July 1961

It rained telegrams after winning that fight – with my daughter, Wendy

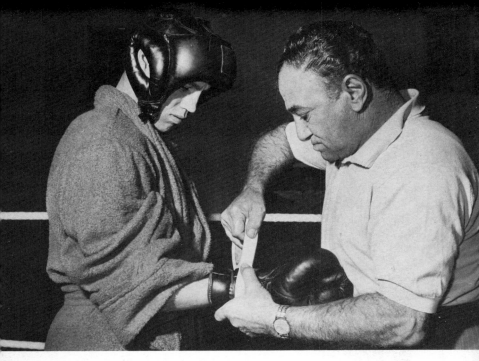

Johnny Dunne gloves me up for sparring in September 1962

On the way to a hollow victory over the great
Sugar Ray Robinson at Wembley later that month

Exchanging punches with Willie the Wisp – my last fight, in 1964

My first acting part,
with Barbara Windsor, in the film
A Study in Terror, in 1965

Arriving in Singapore to film *Five
Ashore*, with Sean Flynn who is
holding a briefcase

weak at the weight. Had I been as strong as a bull, Allen might have out-fiddled me because he'd made up his mind to do it.

But after eight rounds referee Pat Floyd gave Allen the points verdict. The fight was almost last on the programme—there had been a bigger upset when Peter Waterman lost to Boswell St. Louis—and there was some booing of the decision. I couldn't have cared less. I was just pleased the fight was over. I didn't blame anyone but myself for being beaten, though I still don't think he landed enough punches to win. But Allen was good enough to have pinched the points. Good luck to him. Others thought it was a terrible set-back.

I did get some consolation when *Boxing News* wrote: 'Les Allen, who finished in a state of near collapse, with a busted nose and cut eye, was adjudged by referee Pat Floyd to have outpointed Terry Downes. It seemed an astounding decision, and nobody appeared more surprised than Allen. Downes forced the fight from Paddington to Penzance.'

I remembered there was a bit of a rumpus, but what's the use of moaning? With me it was a matter of getting on with the next business. It was up to my managers to get me back. Before I knew it I had earned £700 in two fights, and over £1,000, a grand, in six weeks.

I'd only been boxing pro eight months. That's what makes me laugh when people tell me it's a mug's game. Sure it's hard, but where else could a guy like me have copped that kinda money without thieving?

I went back to Harringay on December 10, matched in a nice £300 job against George Lavery, of Belfast. Something must have gone wrong in that fight. I actually won by a knock-out! Maybe Lavery had been reading my good write-ups and wasn't feeling too brave, but the way I threw a million punches nobody got knocked out. Lavery was an exception. A left hook to the jaw did it in the fifth. I was much too fast and fit for him. It was just a breeze fight. I didn't take the win too seriously.

At that time I still went regularly to watch fights but wasn't as noisy as I am now. I was keeping my eye on the champion, Pat McAteer, from Birkenhead, who was making trips to

America. Eventually Pat retired and emigrated to the States. So most of my training and the matches being sought were with an eye on a title fight with McAteer.

After the loss to Allen and practically unnoticed win over Lavery they got me back in the limelight with my first live TV fight from my favourite joint, Shoreditch Town Hall, again. The opponent was Hamouda Bouraoui, of Tunisia. I had more trouble saying his name then fighting him.

I was supposed to have fought Jean Poisson, but he'd 'done' a hand in training and this wog geezer came in. He was a right hard case and awkward, a typical Continental-style fighter. He covered up well, but was a bit slow and I was able to sink plenty of punches in. It was an entertaining enough fight and, as usual, I took my share of punches. But the other fellah's nose started to swell up and I could see he'd be swallowing the fight before much longer. But I couldn't bung him down, except for a punch that made him half slip over in the fourth. He went back to the corner and they couldn't get him off his stool. His nose was in a bad enough state. It was a handy win, hardly worth the £300, but I wasn't giving any back. To my surprise, Steve Fagan, in the *Daily Sketch*, wrote that Bouraoui was probably my classiest opponent to date. For this fight I was unmarked and had paced myself a lot better. Ryder had kept drilling me. And I was aware, at times, about impressing on the telly.

I wasn't mad about the performance, but Gerard Walter, in the *News Chronicle*, reckoned it the best form I'd shown since turning pro.

I was pleased with the set-up. Sam Burns had joined Ryder in the corner and they spoke my language. I'd get no sympathy from them if I did things wrong, and, more important, they could read the opposition pretty well. I got a laugh watching Sam stalking up and down the dressing-room beforehand, a bag of nerves, and telling me not to worry about being on television and all that.

What with him smoking like a trooper and Jarvis stacking himself up with pills, I'd got a couple of managers who were suffering more than me. Some people reckon they look a pair of hard nuts, but really they're always concerned about their fighters' success. And so they should be!

I'd got acclimatized in England again and almost forgotten the five different years I'd spent in the States. I didn't have much of a break for Christmas, 1957, because I was back in action at Shoreditch on January 7, 1958. The crowds were still pouring in and this small-hall experience shaped my career. It was a smart move. Serge Leveque, who had boxed a draw for the light-heavyweight championship of France, was signed. At that stage I had trouble getting home opponents. I took £160 for wages, which was a drop, but still very high for Shoreditch. Leveque was twenty-nine, and a stonemason from Paris. He'd had thirty-five fights, seven losses. I gave away 4 lb.

I'd realized that I'd have to stop the whirlwind stuff that was needed to get three-round amateur decisions. I'd started settling the pace and picking punches better. Ryder had done a good job. And the Press were flattering with comments on the new look. I parried plenty of the Froggy's punches, too, and came out without a blemish. I hardly recognized myself with a clean face after the fight.

When I put Leveque down I turned to the corner for their approval, but saw Sam and Tom chatting away. They were congratulating themselves on the way I'd done it. I told them they'd better keep their eye on me next time in case I was calling for help. Anyway, Leveque went down four times in four rounds and was stopped gasping for breath. I'd belted him around the ribs, which wasn't to his or the referee's liking, but certainly was to mine. It was a lucky thirteenth fight.

Watching from the ringside was Freddie Cross, a Welshman from Bermondsey, whom I was matched with twenty days later at Harringay. This was really an important fight. Cross had been rated above me, was a fair boxer, and beating him put me in line to fight McAteer. Solomons paid up £450 for my end of the purse, which was terrific money. We were only a supporting bout on a big bill.

In the big one Dave Charnley was fighting American Don Jordan, who went on to win the world welter-weight title. I was more or less getting the corner crew organized and because my style demanded risks they carried enough potions to patch-up a slaughtered bull. Mickey Duff and Tom knew how to gee me up—though I didn't need much reminding to get on with the business.

The potions weren't enough that night. I lost to Cross at the end of the sixth when referee Jack Hart reckoned the cuts both below and above my right eye were bad enough. I sat on my stool knowing I was the better man, but shrugged off the blow. We'd cracked heads like billiard balls and Cross had a cut cheekbone, but when I bled I did it in full Technicolor and the ref had to step in.

Cross put up a good show, and all that, he'd scarpered away using a good left hand to stop me boring in. For two rounds he was doing pretty good. But I really turned on the pressure in the third because I could see something had to be done. The corner were giving me hell. Cross wasn't moving so fast by the fifth, but my cuts brought a desperate fight-back from him. Again the Press called it one of the best fights of the season. We had the crowd hopping about as usual.

While the crowd were still roaring at the finish Solomons came up on the ring apron and said he'd make the return fight for February 25. But we never fought again. Cross went out of the picture.

'Downes seemed a little unlucky, for he seemed slightly ahead', said *Boxing News*. 'If Downes never has worse luck than he did against Cross he can still call himself unfortunate', said the *Daily Sketch*. 'Downes was a desperately unlucky loser . . . he came out of a clinch with his right eye looking like a burst tomato', said the *Daily Mirror*. So I'd lost no prestige and I took the defeat in my stride because I was convinced I could always lick Cross.

The only regret I had was not having the cuts stitched. I never made the mistake again. When they cleaned me up the damage didn't look too bad, so Tom taped the cuts together. But during the night the plaster must have loosened and, because of that, I've still got those criss-Cross scars

My skin heals pretty well—it knows we need the money!—

and I was ready for another fight within a month. Instead of Cross I was matched with Dennis Booty, of Stepney, the same guy I'd had to pay to spar with me when I was an amateur. From what I'd seen of him in that sparring session made me sure I'd win. And I was getting another £450 to prove it!

But Booty had been doing well as a pro, was a good banger, and had knocked over a few fair fighters. So they had no trouble 'selling' this fight. Booty had a big following and it caused a lot of argument among the supporters. But never for a second did I consider I couldn't win. The big fight was Willie Pastrano versus Brian London.

Despite my face now being a bit scarred (I'd started pickling it to keep me pretty) I waded into Booty to get him out of the way early just in case accidents happened and I was cut again. It turned out to be one-way, with Booty going down. I had him flat on his face, from a cracking uppercut, in the second. In the third I switched to the ribs and bunged him down again. He was out on his feet and the fight was over. Although he was a good whacker I hadn't sampled many and it was better than working for a living.

By the way, Dick Tiger also appeared on the programme, but didn't make much impression or get much publicity beating Johnny Read again. It was just another fight.

I started stacking some money away, because I could visualize I was going to be getting into the big-time if this luck kept up.

Three weeks later they sorted me out a quieter fight at Leyton Baths against another Tunisian, Ben Farhat. He'd boxed a draw with Les Allen, who had beaten me, and had had twenty-six fights. He'd also been sparring with German Gustav Scholz, so I reckoned he knew the game. But to the betting-boys he was just another mug for my build-up. And even matchmaker Duff kidded me it was an easy job.

But it shows how wrong you can be. I beat Farhat, but I came out with a gashed lip, two loose teeth, and a busted eye. If that was what I was in for against the mugs, God help me, I thought, when I started fighting the top men. I came out of the ring that night and called to Duff, 'Is that your idea of an

G

easy job?' But often these hard and underrated geezers give more trouble than accomplished fighters. With my walk-in style nothing was easy. Maybe I'd made hard work of it. In the second round he lifted my legs clean off the canvas with a cracking right and, thanks very much, I'm laying down like a good 'un. I didn't even remember being hit. I heard the referee calling three, four, and thought I'd better not lay about any longer.

I managed to tear in and stop him from finishing me off and I think this come-back took some of the guts out of him. But my corner was considering pulling me out because the cut lip was bad. With a mixture of blood, vaseline, and the taste of the gumshield, my mouth tasted like a bus-driver's glove.

Again in the fourth Farhat had sent over another right-hander and I've stood for it again. I'm back on the floor and this was getting boring. This was some mug they'd dug up for me. So I more or less forgot about whatever defence I was supposed to have and just stood there slinging punches. He was banging back and again the local punters were getting their value. He practically fell off his stool going back after the fourth and I thought that was a handy sign.

Farhat's two London agents, Roger Colson and Dick Reekie, who had plenty of practice reviving the fighters they brought to England, had to force him off the stool for the fifth. I darted over to his corner while they were still pushing him off, snarling at him like a wrestler. He turned his face and buried it in his gloves, facing out of the ring. I thought this was handy and just whipped in a few punches for good measure before I heard the referee yelling 'Enough' and accepting Farhat's surrender.

Considering he'd done such a good job putting me on the deck—it was one of the best punches I've taken—I couldn't understand why Farhat packed it in. I'd just out-gamed him.

It wasn't the kind of fight I'd expected to bring any real rewards—but Astaire and Burns did a feat. They got me a fight with champion McAteer at Harringay on April 15, 1958. What a break this was. It was to be an overweight match, but if I did well I'd get a straight shot at the title. That meant I'd step over the other challengers. But that man Dick Tiger turned up again. He took the Empire title off McAteer at Liverpool and Pat was injured. My fight was off.

Instead, Solomons matched me with Tuzo (Kid) Portuguez, from Costa Rica. To the public he was just another opponent. It wasn't so much who I was beating but *how* I was doing it.

But I knew the score of Portuguez because I'd seen him fighting when I was in the States. He was thirty-one and had been around for a long time, with eighty fights, which wasn't bad considering I had just completed my first pro year. I'd seen the tough Portuguez battling away with the likes of Joey Giardello, Joey Giambra, Randy Sandy, and Willie Troy in the States. So I really reckoned him.

But as it turned out it was a bit pitiful. He fought like he'd come over to England just for the money. He was carrying plenty of lead in his legs. Because he didn't offer much resistance I fought badly too. I bunged him down in the second, which was a feat, considering the punchers he'd met, but I wasn't going to try to finish him. As it happened, the bell saved him.

While a lot of people were raving about my punching, in my heart I knew I wasn't a big puncher. That's why I throw a million of them to make them count. I figured I'd only bang up my hands if I tried knocking-out Portuguez. Much better bangers than me in the States couldn't do it. It was probably my dullest fight to date, maybe because I had too much respect for the old guy.

But some fighters always come along and make bad fights. For all I know, Greb or Mickey Walker might have made hard work of a fellah like Portuguez. Anyway, I well won the eight-round points and, while I didn't expect the critics to be raving about me, I consoled myself laughing all the way to the bank. I'd copped nearly £2,500 from November to March and I was well pleased with myself making £4,000 or more with seventeen fights after only twelve months. I'd been licked and cut, yet I'd still managed to get the experience I wanted.

What I hadn't bothered to scream about while I was training for the Portuguez fight was a pulled back muscle. I thought maybe I'd sat in a draught or just ricked it, but sometimes the pain was real bad. A Board of Control doctor gave me an injection to make sure I'd be recovered for the fight, but the thought the pain may come back bothered me. That's why I think I'd more or less made up my mind that I'd win on points. I was half pulling some punches in case my back went in the fight.

It turned out that this complaint nearly crippled me when I challenged Paul Pender for the world title in Boston.

On June 3, 1958, Solomons pulled off the match with McAteer. This time it went on at White City, where Solomons staged some fantastic open-air shows. I've never seen better-presented shows. My eight-rounder, again a non-title, was billed below Joe Erskine v. Brian London for the heavy-weight championship; Dave Charnley v. Joey Lopes, of America; and Mike Holt v. Yolande Pompey. Ringside seats were a fiver.

I got £600 for the fight, but I'd have taken it for sixpence, because this was the chance I'd wanted. The White City set-up was great, with a long walk to the ringside, and I revelled in the tension that built up. I love the feeling of having the people sitting on the edges of their seats. I couldn't stand the thought of the fans being stuck in the bar when I was fighting. So long as they'd paid to get in I suppose I shouldn't have cared less, but when the call came to go on I came out of the tunnel that led from the dressing-room to the middle of the grass pitch feeling real good.

I'd got accustomed to the betting-boys who scarpered around the ringsides, though there were notices everywhere that no betting was allowed. Sometimes I'd hear the same voice cheering for both fighters. He'd switched bets and was earning whichever way the fight went.

A lot of people reckon the betting-boys are a nuisance. Well, I've often got more amusement watching them root a fighter home than watching the fights. They are the backbone of the game, and create atmosphere like bookies on a racecourse. Without them the game would be dead.

I was in the ring early against McAteer. It was still daylight. He was a good-looking fellah, with dark wavy hair, and by the look of him hadn't been hit too much. The only time I'd seen

McAteer perform I was his biggest supporter—and suffered for it. When I was back in Baltimore, Pat Mac was in the States to fight Spider Webb, in Chicago, and when the fight came on TV I got a bit of the old British loyalty back and was sticking my money up on McAteer.

I got a right going-over from all the Marines, who were calling the Limeys all sorts of so-and-so's when Mac was done up in two rounds. But Webb was a bit special—as I was to find out.

McAteer had won the title in 1955 by a foul against Johnny Sullivan, another guy who'd done a lot of fighting in the States. McAteer went through forty fights without defeat—which is a feat—before a South African, Jimmy Elliott, out-pointed him. But it was a tragedy for Elliott. A year later McAteer went to South Africa and stopped him in six rounds. Elliott died after the fight. I was shocked when they said Elliott, who'd fought in Britain, had been given a licence to fight after having an operation in Holland for a detached retina. I reckoned somebody had blundered.

Anyway, the announcements over with, I went after McAteer to stop him settling down and dictating his pace. Despite the appearance that I was scurrying all over the place, I wasn't exactly a mug at the boxing lark. I was well pleased with the way the fight went. I was often out-jabbing him, which was Mac's game. I was turning hooks to head and body off my straight jabs. Maybe the open air made me move faster, but certainly the champ was creaking by comparison.

Because of the cold and the occasion I gave the crowd a bigger war-dance at the off and one of the reporters said the time would come when I'd knock myself out with this act. McAteer hardly laid a glove on me to bother and his face was puffed and bruised, which made a nice change for me.

I suppose McAteer was realizing before the fight was over that he'd come to the end of the road. The points decision for me was a formality. They'd have lynched the ref if he'd given it the other way. Beating the champion was a right feat and I figured I'd easily nick the title off him the next time we fought. I changed quickly and was back watching the show when M.C. Johnny Best—who had promoted most of McAteer's fights in Liverpool—announced that the champion had retired.

McAteer went into the ring to take a bow and I stood among the crowd clapping him, though I was choked that my chance to fight him for the title had gone. He seemed a nice, clean-cut fellah and I respected him for retiring. He could have made about £3,000 to defend against me, but with a pride I had to admire he went out rather than chance being humiliated. Good luck to him. I never saw McAteer again.

Because boxing was my business I'd spend hours reading the small print of record-books and scanning papers for middle-weight results around the world. While Burns and Astaire had more experience, they were also handling fighters at other weights and I didn't expect them to be on the ball with the middle-weight results as I was.

So we more or less had an understanding that I'd be consulted before any foreign fighters were lined-up for me. It wasn't that I wanted to manage them, but I considered myself a shrewd enough judge and knew all the names. It made a good set-up for us.

Eighteen fights and I was ready to move into the big stuff. The fighting I'd done with the good class in the Marines made up for lack of experience here. But, understandably, my managers weren't going to go mad. So another work-out was picked for Streatham Ice Rink in July. He was Algerian Constant Alcantara, who sounded more like a Soho waiter than a fighter. I've seen waiters who looked like they might give me more trouble.

After I'd tumbled Alcantara couldn't fight too much, I waded in unmercifully and by the third round he'd quit. They dragged him off the floor when the bell saved him after the third. We'd been punching inside and I whipped over two good hooks that half the crowd didn't see—and poor old Constant was among that half. When his seconds retired him the Algerian didn't 'arf look relieved. He hugged me like a brother.

I got £400. People were getting a stretch at the Old Bailey for less villainy. This was better than thieving money. Having earned a few quid, I had already gone into business on my own account, without being pushed, having half-share with cousin Pat in a second-hand-car showroom at Stonebridge. We called it Speedway Motors. Because I'd invested money in the little house I needed to borrow some off my managers. I figured that's what managers are for. The showroom would cost £3,000. It held twelve cars.

When I explained what I wanted the cash for to Astaire, whose business is everything, including property, he sent a man to look at the shop and didn't reckon it worth the money. But I wouldn't be swayed. So he loaned me the money. Between training spells I'd take over while Pat went out searching for cars and I conditioned myself for business checking the books and we always managed to make a week's wages.

Later we took over another site at Manor Road, opposite the house I'd bought. Without any advice, Pat and me had a go.

With the British title vacant, Solomons did a smart bit of matchmaking, pairing me with Phil Edwards, of Cardiff, and applying to the Board for it to be recognized for the title. They agreed. Freddie Cross put up a bit of a scream, but it didn't count. So in twenty fights I'd made it. Edwards, whose real name was Cilia, was a well-built, nice-looking geezer who'd found a lot of support. He started clear favourite. He'd been fighting as a pro since he was sixteen with fifty-one fights in five years, compared to my fifteen months. He was a smart boxer and even looked stronger than me.

But I'd kept Edwards under a microscope, as it were, for a long time. I'd watched him work—that's the word we fighters use for fighting—and I'd never had even the slightest worry about beating him. For one thing, I didn't think he could punch too good because he looked a bit muscle-bound. But I had to respect his all-round ability because of his experience.

He'd given Dick Tiger a good fight after me, and the Press were nearly all tipping him. Some of them thought I'd blow-up before fifteen rounds. I'd only boxed eight rounds. They reckoned I couldn't keep my pace up against a man of Edwards's class. They'd forgotten about the years of spade-work for stamina in the Marines.

Tell the truth, I considered Edwards a routine fight because I wasn't doing anything special in the way of training.

I couldn't punish my body any more than I had been doing for years. I'd rigged up a weight of 15 lb. and had it tied in a sling to my head, like wearing a medal around the head instead of neck, and used this to strengthen my neck and jaw. I called it the Pendulum. I ran like a cross-country athlete. I could sprint pretty good and run backwards faster than some guys could go forward. I worked in the gym with dumb-bells (somebody said they reminded me of some of my opponents) and had a good mob of sparring-partners and paid £200 for their services. But I refused to train away from home because I was happy and taking no liberties. Barbara's courtship suffered, because if I called on her I left like a lark, without a lark, to be in bed by 9.30. She was going half crazy because I don't think she believed I was always going straight home. We had started talking wedding contracts at the time and I guarantee the wedding was on and off more times than a water-tap.

I told Barbara I must win the title first. Now I was stymied. I knew I'd beat Edwards and then I couldn't find any more alibis. I was nabbed—and loved it.

The big-fight weighing-in went without any hitches and there wasn't much to separate us. He was about a quarter-pound heavier. The official top-liner was a return between Willie Pastrano and Brian London and I was tickled pink sharing a dressing-room with Pastrano. It sorta gave me a bit of class.

On Pastrano's previous fights in Britain I hadn't pushed myself up front and made myself busy about when he refereed me in Miami. To him I was just another fighter, but we had a good old chat while we put the ring togs on that night. Angelo Dundee, his trainer, of course, was there. So I felt like I was back in the States again.

This time I got a real big fanfare and the spotlight treatment, and jazzed all down the aisle and gave 'em the old routine with a vengeance. I was so sure I could set a fast pace and keep going that I waded in, as usual, from the first bell. I daresay Edwards had been told to take it easy while I fired away and burned out. That suited me, because I'd be sure of grabbing a good lead and he wasn't 'arf going to be choked when I kept punching away in the later rounds.

I wasn't going to just wing away at Edwards and hope for the best. I knew I could box and punch a bit better than him, and fight a lot harder if I had to. And that's how it turned out. He was a good jabber, but I out-jabbed him. In the second round I caught him a beauty of a right-hander on the chops and I don't know what held him up, but he certainly did some funny things standing up. They said later that that punch altered the pattern of the fight, but I couldn't understand why. If I'd taken the punch instead of landing it, for me the pattern would still have been the same. I had a bit too much edge all round.

By the half-way mark I was loving it and there wasn't a mark on me. Poor old Phil's face was chopping up bad. It wasn't a great fight, but hard. We were well matched, but the further the fight went, the more Edwards had to soak-up. If I'd been able to whack just that bit harder I'd have done Phil a favour by knocking him out. As it was, he just had to keep going until referee Bill Williams flung himself between us in the thirteenth round and hauled me off. Like the good fighter he was, Edwards hadn't gone down—but he was well and truly punched out. I was the new champion of Great Britain. Date: September 30, 1958.

While the referee was trying to grab my arm to raise it— like anyone didn't know who'd won!—I was pulling him with me because I was bent on sorting out two of the writers who'd gone out on a limb and tipped Edwards to win.

I spotted Reg Gutteridge at the press-table, and with the ref half-raising my arm, I called out, 'How's that for stamina?' and laughed: 'That'll teach you!' While my seconds were scrambling around ready to lift me up, I spotted Peter Wilson, who'd written that Edwards ought to be too smart. He got the same treatment. But they both took it well. I'd been so sure of winning that I'd saved up that bit for something to please me more. It's so great to prove people wrong.

They pinned the Lonsdale Belt around me and, I'm telling

you, it was marvellous. I felt ten feet tall. Not even a bit of my blood spilt, either. Mum and Barbara, who couldn't resist getting into the act, were scrambling up the corner steps to start kissing me. When you think of it, it's a stupid time for love and kisses, but the occasion is so unforgettable anything goes. Me, a champion. I didn't even care about getting the sweat or grease on Barbara's coat. It cost a tenner—but who's counting? I got £1,500 gross purse.

They brought the TV cameras in the dressing-room and under those big lamps they couldn't find much wrong with my face that couldn't be straightened out. I made my little speech, which 'arf the people north of Paddington Station probably couldn't understand, but I meant well.

I went on to wish Edwards luck and say what a good fight it had been, and he looked like a steamroller had gone over him. I daresay the bumps and bruises would have gone down in a couple of days. But the referee couldn't wait that long. He was a nice fellah and not so long after the fight I went down to Cardiff for a bit of car business and Edwards insisted I met him for a cup of tea. And if that doesn't take the cake, when Edwards eventually retired—after we'd been through the fight all over again—he took over a Cardiff café and had a 5 ft. tall cut-out cardboard posed figure of me at the doorway. Maybe it was just to keep the cats away.

My family and a few mates decided we'd celebrate at the Jack O'Club's in Brewer Street, Soho, owned by Jack Isow, who is a right character and plays host to famous fighters and show-business stars. His game is insulting his customers. None of them ever hit back because old Jack is such a roly-poly guy that if he fell over he'd very likely rock himself to sleep trying to get up.

Here's a guy who'd cause a bit of a stir if he ever wrote a book about life in the West End. Something like a 'Soho—so what' title would suit him. Anyway, I'll back us Cockneys when it comes to a bit of jollification and a good old knees-up.

At the fight I'd seen Ingemar Johansson, a right good-looking Swede who was European heavy-weight champion at the time and went on to win the world title. Ingo's bingo right-hand was doing fine holding the hand of his future wife Birgit—and what a cracker she is—while they watched Pastrano and London.

Actually, he didn't fight in England and didn't fight Brian London until 1963—Ingo's last fight. Somehow we blagged Johansson down the club, and before I knew it the hounds, my mates, had got him doing the old knees-up like a good 'un. I could see by the way the booze was flowing and everyone was dancing that this shindig would go on until dawn, so I blew home early.

On the way back the ham actor in me couldn't resist buying the early editions of the morning papers. I'd got a terrific Press. In capital letters the *Daily Mirror* said 'Downes was a Revelation'. Peter Wilson reported: 'The kid who had never fought more than eight rounds before was expected to crumble after the half-way stage. In fact that's when he really came into his own . . . this same sort of style made former world champion "Homicide" Henry Armstrong one of the most difficult men to beat.' Me? Compared to Henry Armstrong. I loved it.

The *Daily Mail* said: 'Terry Downes, the Paddington boy who learned to fight the tough American way in the U.S. Marines, is the new British middle champion . . . he battered Phil Edwards into thirteen rounds of defeat so complete that the referee had to walk in and save Edwards from a hiding that had become almost too painful to watch. Edwards had his face cut and carved into a grotesque mask. Both his eyes had great bruises around them. His nose was squashed, his mouth agape and bleeding. It was the most thorough beating a man can take without going down.' From where I saw Edwards he didn't look quite that bad, but I've gotta admit he was a bit of a mess.

The *Daily Herald* said: '. . . one of the most savage fights I have ever seen in this class. If Downes goes on fighting like this he will be our best middle champion since Turpin.'

Said the *Evening News*: 'Downes found the energy to address the crowd, pose and revel in the pageantry of Lonsdale Belt presentation, and poke his head outside the ropes to remind me of "having the nerve" to tip Edwards.'

I lapped up every word.

The next day Barbara practically stole the publicity with whacking big pictures of her wiping my face, smiling, and sitting on the bonnet of one of my cars-for-sale.

Life was champion—but I had to think about getting hitched. I'd promised Barbara a championship for a wedding present and we put the banns up for December 21 at St. Saviour's Church, Warwick Avenue, Paddington. I'd signed on the dotted line. . . .

Getting a New Face

I'D SUNK some more cash into buying and selling cars and getting accustomed to dealing with the public. When it came to flogging a motor I didn't have all that front. I usually worked that job on to Pat while I fiddled around dusting here and there or picking up cars for selling. If we bought an old job my dad and Pat's dad would hover around it like flies round a jam-pot. They've loved tinkling about with engines, and the older the engine the better. Abbott and Costello, we used to call 'em.

Pat and me thought an open site, at that time, was better than a showroom and we bought a pitch in Manor Road.

Meanwhile I had my eye on a £5,000 fight with Frenchman Charlie Humez for the European title. He was a real good performer coming to the end of his career. But he'd already signed to defend against the German Gustav Scholz. If Humez won I was guaranteed the next shot for the big money. But the chump goes and gets himself done by Scholz, in Berlin, and retired. Why didn't I fight Scholz? It would have been a big draw, but at the time British promoters wouldn't book a German fighter. They feared a ringside boycott from the Jewish fraternity. A few Germans have crept into England in the past few years, but Solomons and Harry Levene still haven't booked them.

So to expand my business interests—and I was still going it alone—I bought a tipper-lorry for carting demolition, coal, or any other goods. The game was to get a 'B' licence, which enabled you to do this work. Just having the licence made the sale of the lorry a profitable deal. I'd heard that if you grafted well a lorry could bring in a half-hundred quid a week, but you had to advertise that you were applying for the licence in case somebody objected because you were stealing a living from them.

I applied for the licences and got them first go—without an objection. So I bought three lorries. One of my drivers was Johnny Berry, the boxer I'd seen at Wembley Town Hall and who'd become a good spar-mate. He turned out the best driver I'd got. The reason why people made money was because they drove their own lorries, took decent care of them. But the moment I hired staff the troubles started. They'd have a break-down and sit all day waiting for help. Or they'd cost a fortune in insurance banging about into other cars.

My uncle took a lorry home—and it was stolen. And a good job, too, I thought. But when we checked the insurance it only covered for the lorry being in the garage. So we'd done £2,000 in cold blood. I didn't feel *two grand*. I'd spilt some hot blood to get it. This business, I thought, was a hard game. I used to buy tons of hardcore, but Pat and me would have to climb on walls of derelict houses to bang them down. We had a lorry with an automatic shovel.

Tell the truth, I'd enjoyed all the graft, provided the weather kept fine. I had a lot of fun at it. Maybe it wasn't exactly champion work, but it made a living. But if Astaire and Burns had known I was dangling on roofs they'd have thrown a fit. They thought I was laying about in a car saleroom all day.

But with the aggravation of staff and expenses we decided to sell up. As it turned out, we didn't do any financial damage, even with the blow of the nicked lorry.

Being the champ entitled me to a slightly longer rest. I took a whole month out. (What a walkover it is for heavy-weight champions who fight once a year!) But because I wanted to show a bit of thanks to the crowd at Shoreditch, where they'd given me encouragement, I showed off in an exhibition there. The promoter, Harry Grossmith, who'd been around the fight-game for thirty-odd years, bought me a watch inscribed: 'From the fans of Shoreditch. Thanking you for the many thrills and wishing you best of luck for the future.'

The Mayor of Shoreditch made the presentation. I really was tickled pink. 'My Own' had given me something to remember them by.

On November 4, 1958, as a warm-up for Fireworks Night, I was matched with another tongue-twisting Continental, Mohammed Taibi, of Morocco, at Seymour Hall, Marylebone. But this was a show with a difference. The promoter was an attractive woman! To officially sign contracts I went out to meet Mrs. Monica Springer, who was only twenty-nine, at her beautiful home in Hampstead. Now this was the way I reckoned all fight business should be done.

Mrs. Springer was in a committee of women, including Astaire's wife Phyllis, who were working for children's charities. I knew Taibi was only a work-out—but the place was packed. Taibi, who was twenty-five, was a motor mechanic managed by Gaston Charles-Raymond, who'd produced world champions. Taibi's claim to fame was never being stopped in thirty-four fights. I'd never let a Continental go the limit. And poor old Mohammed, whatever they called him, took a bit of a larruping. I nearly tore him in half with some body punches and he held on tight. But in the third the referee stopped it.

Taibi had lost his last couple of fights, so stopping him didn't mean much. Tell the truth, it was a bit of a liberty. He wasn't in my class. Never mind, the money was handy and the Mayor of Paddington presented me with a silver cigarette box.

But the big kick I got out of this fight was a plug in the *Sunday Pictorial* from Tommy Farr, who, after all, was a great fighter and must have been a good judge. He wrote: 'Take the hit-or-be-hit style of Jock McAvoy, mix it with the ready-to-laugh-at-himself humour of Max Baer and there you have British middle-weight champion Terry Downes, the best 11 st. 6 lb. man in Europe. . . . What a strange mixture this Downes is. He doesn't claim to be an intellectual, but he studies his boxing like an eager undergraduate. Terry is aware that lovers of orthodox boxing accuse him of taking two punches to land one. He shrugs that off with "I'm in the ring to entertain. If I wanted to do a slow fox-trot I'd go to a dance-hall.". . . '

Although Barbara and me were rushing around making

wedding plans, with arguments and me getting the ring back every two minutes, I still had to stay in good shape to appear as champion for the first time at Wembley, the Empire Pool, where Solomons had moved to share dates with Levene because Harringay had been closed down.

I knew my opponent would be an American for December 9—only twelve days before the church date that was making me much more nervous. I had no idea who I'd be fighting, but while I was skipping in the gym somebody said I was wanted on the phone. Normally I'd never stop sweating to answer a call, but they said it was Solomons. Only for him would I have stopped. He said he'd get either Spider Webb or Gene Fullmer.

I went back to skipping twice as hard, thrilled to bits. I knew the pair of them were top men and hard nuts. At the time I'd have fought Sonny Liston. This was a chance I'd wanted—to get in the ring with a real good American fighter. I knew beating home opponents wouldn't mean much in America, so beating Webb or Fullmer would make my mark. I couldn't see either of them as a bad match for me. I've made cracks since about offering me Webb or Fullmer was like saying 'Do you want to be hanged or shot?' but that's because I've learned since that sometimes it's better to go round a high wall than over it.

But I trained like a madman and they couldn't get Fullmer, probably because he cut pretty easily and figured he wouldn't get any favours from a referee in Britain. So Webb was signed. I'd seen him fight, of course, in the States and knew he was a bit tasty. My brother-in-law, Jimmy Hines, was in London from Baltimore and he knew the strength of Webb. Jimmy was a cigarette salesman at home, but he kept in shape with a bit of boxing. So I copped him for a bit of sparring, too.

Having remembered Webb tuning-up McAteer, I reckoned I'd get the money I'd bet in the Marines back and a bit of revenge if I could stop Spider, who was an intelligent coloured guy hoping to be a cop. He came over to London with Carl Nelson, a Chicago police sergeant who had been a bodyguard for Joe Louis. Did Louis really need a bodyguard?

The Press were saying I'd taken on too much. But I couldn't see it. Because Webb had whipped McAteer didn't make him King Kong, but I knew Webb's ten-round tanning of Dick Tiger was handy form. 'This is a bad match for young Downes', wrote Peter Wilson. 'Downes is overmatched', said Don Saunders. 'I hate to say it, but I think Downes is in for a man-sized licking', said Ernie Jarvis. 'Downes always gives a hundred per cent show, but this is hardly enough, after two years of pro boxing, to put him against the world's best', said Harold Mayes.

I'd seen Webb fight six times and, as far as I knew, most writers hadn't seen him perform. I'd pickled my hands in witches' brew, after training, which stunk the joint out. It was a concoction of raw lemons, spices and brine. The bare-knuckle boys used to pickle themselves and I reckon you can't beat the old remedies. My hands were hardening. I was ready for the world.

The fight was my first solo top-liner at a big show and the Empire Pool was packed. The fight had certainly caught on and Solomons didn't miss a trick with his publicity. He had a sell-out. A lot of American fighters on the slide had been brought to England over the years, but we all knew Webb was at his peak. He had had thirty-four fights in five years and was ranked World No. 3. He might have been champion if Ray Robinson and Carmen Basilio hadn't been playing see-saw with the title.

When I bounced into the ring at Wembley you could have cut the air with a knife. Honest, the atmosphere was terrific. Everyone seemed on the edges of their seats before we'd started. Tom Ryder had trouble pulling my gown over my scarlet gloves and I remember looking down to a reporter at the press bench and saying, 'I think Tom's half boozed.' It all helped to ease the tenseness.

A half-drunk supporter came rushing up the corner steps to give me a bit of a cuddle, and breathed all over me. I couldn't have a go at the geezer. He was only being matey, so I said, 'I know the place is a sell-out, mate, but you can't nick my seat!' I think Tom and Sam Burns were too nervous to laugh, but I was really excited to get going.

H

But the excitement was knocked out of me almost from the first bell. I walked into a smashing right-hander that made me feel the canvas had been whipped from under me. I was peering out the ring to a hundred eyes, probably looking for a friendly pair, when I heard the referee call 'Three'. I managed to pull my legs up and kneel for eight seconds. They were calling out in my corner to keep my arms up and move. I was up in a bit of cloud and don't really remember staying out of trouble for the rest of the round.

Webb was a hellava fighter and nailed me some good shots. I thought maybe the writers were right. But I wasn't going to swallow it. When the first-round bell went I stayed on my feet somehow and flopped on the stool thinking this was going to be some fight. Somebody said, 'Never mind, the crowd is with you, Tel.' I was thinking I wished I was with them!

As I went out for the second I gritted my teeth and thought, 'Tel, you'll have to do something a bit special, mate,' and walked into Webb like I didn't reckon him. I belted him with a peach of a right-hander, which at least brought a bit of respect, but before the round was over I'd got a graze over the left eye. He'd also ripped home some uppercuts. The going was hard.

But in the next few rounds we tore each other apart, and in the fourth, which turned out my best round, I had him backing off. The crowd were going raving mad. They say there hadn't been atmosphere and excitement like it since Turpin licked Robinson. By the fifth I'd punched myself out a bit, but knew if I took a breather I'd come back with plenty of reserve. By the look of Webb he was in worse shape than me. He was blowing like a good 'un and I cracked him in the mouth to make his gumshield come spinning out.

In the sixth my gumshield went flying and my nose started to bleed hard. They couldn't stem the blood from the eye-cut that had worsened. Yet for my money it was still touch-and-go and whoever could pull out the most would win the fight.

I'd hit Webb enough to make him start shaking his head, which was a bad sign from an experienced fighter. He was definitely flagging. But after the seventh the referee, Eugene Henderson, came to my corner and looked at the cuts. 'I'm all right, Ref,' I said. 'He's worse than me.' So I went out for the eighth knowing I'd have to throw everything in case the cuts got too bad.

When both eyebrows were cut I knew things were getting dodgy. Seeing the blood, naturally, gave Webb a bit more heart and after he'd soaked up some stick from the earlier rounds he pulled out enough just when he looked beaten. That's the thing about great fighters. Webb was able to do that.

At the end of the round Henderson again came to my corner for a roll-call and I could see Webb pushing his manager out of the way in his corner to see what was going on. He was dying for the ref to stop the fight. I know, because that's how fighters react in a tough situation. Seeing Webb act like that made me even more wild that I wanted to go on. But trainer Tom was looking a bit worried and I suppose the referee could see he wasn't going to argue. I saw Henderson wave his hands to say 'That's enough' and I was off the stool protesting. I'd never felt so upset in my life. I thought I could have gone on. I might even have won it.

When I saw Webb in the dressing-room afterwards I was sure I could have won. I'd been patched up, showered, and dressed to go home while he was stretched out on the rubbing table still exhausted. He couldn't move. All the reporters were there to prove it.

Barbara and Mum had come rushing up to the corner crying, and I felt like joining in. I was too choked to talk. But I pulled myself together and quipped to Solomons as I left the ring, 'O.K., Jack, when do I fight next?' I was only laughing to stop from crying.

But I put on a front in Webb's dressing-room, saying: 'I hope you come back soon, Spider, because I could do with a return. My manager needs the money.' He was a polite guy, a real pro. I had nothing but respect for him, even if I did think he might have been a bit lucky. Nelson, his handler, looked like he was pleased with the result and admitted he'd thought the fight was going to be a lot easier for Webb.

'We're not saying we don't want a return,' said Nelson, 'but the price would have to be right. This guy Downes is a real fighter. We were issued with a lot of propaganda that Downes was just an eager kid. We're not falling for that stuff again.'

I'd trained hard enough to make me bad-tempered. At home I'd thought about the fight until it had driven me half mad with excitement, but I walked out of Wembley cut-up and choked. You could have put a finger in the width of the cut over my eye. Some of my gilt had gone and I got a couple of thousand quid for my trouble. When I paid off the expenses and the Board of Control's tax—a deduction that annoys me— I figured the money wasn't enough.

I tossed and turned in bed all night wondering about the future—but the terrific fight, and the marvellous press response, took good care of that. Pride was hurt, pay was poor, but I was still wanted. 'Cockney Courage Shocks the Spider', said the *Daily Mirror* heading. 'Bring out the medals! Hang out the flags! Sound the trumpets and proclaim the courage of Cockney Whizz-Kid Terry Downes—Britain's middle-weight champion, and a throwback to the days when raw-fisted Britons fought until they could not see, and then boxed on by braille', wrote Peter Wilson, who also added a warning that hit home: 'I hope that once again we have not crushed a bright star so rapidly that he will burn out like a meteor.'

'Downes stopped—but how Wembley cheered his grit, guts, and gusto!' said the *Daily Mail*. 'Downes beaten—but oh! what a fight', said the *Daily Sketch*.

'Cuts rob Downes', said the *Daily Express* and: 'Downes tried to fight off referee Henderson . . . the scene at the end of the greatest fighting show I have ever seen from any British fighter', wrote Desmond Hackett. 'British boxing will never die so long as we have fighters with the BIG fighting heart of tearaway Terry Downes', said the *Daily Herald*.

These write-ups were a great consolation. Whenever I disagree with something written, or even laugh at it, I always think how fairly the critics treated me for the Webb fight.

Mind you, when Solomons said, the following day, that he'd still planned to match me with Sugar Ray Robinson for the world title, the Press, particularly my ole mate Peter Wilson, didn't 'arf belt the daylights out of the idea. At the time,

maybe, they were right. How were they to know that five
years later I'd be fighting the one and only Sugar Ray—and
cane him!

My next promotion was the contract for life with Barbara.
Because of the boxing bug I'd left arrangements a bit late and
couldn't understand it when we couldn't book a hall for the
reception and booze-up. She got me chasing around like a dog
with two tails—that's the term I'll use in this book but it's
not exactly what I mean—and finally we've only had to go
and change the date! Instead of a Saturday, when most of the
Cockneys have their wedding booze-ups so they can sleep it
off before work, we had to switch to a Sunday.

I was twenty-two, sweating and a bit puffed around the ole
boat-race—the face—and she was nineteen and looked handsome. We had a page-boy rigged out in scarlet-and-gold boxing
gear and the mob that turned up made an arch of boxing
gloves. I must have made a dozen speeches at the Cavendish
Rooms, Willesden. They couldn't keep me down. I had my
managers there, of course, a few newspapermen whom I
considered were matey, some of the amateur club boys, two
fighting families (mobs of 'em)—and Solomons.

Trust Jack to come up with a surprise. He read out a telegram from Sugar Ray Robinson to announce he would be
ready to fight me when the honeymoon was over. What a time
to choose! It was probably the only time in my life I was
concerned about getting away from the fight game. Could you
blame me? I'd found another game not so tough.

We flew to the South of France and I drove Barbara mad
pulling her leg for her first flight. I got her walking in the
middle of the plane aisle to make sure she didn't rock the
plane and she finished up getting locked in the toilet.

For the first time in years I just lazed around, yet all the time
my mind was wondering about fighting. Solomons telephoned
a couple of times, so I couldn't exactly get away from it all. I
also spoke to the managers.

I had a dinner date when I got back with Solomons and his
wife Fay, and a writer and his wife. Bruce Forsyth, the compère
at the London Palladium Sunday night TV show, chatted with

us and asked if I'd fancy going on stage and entering in the 'Beat-the-Clock' game. It was a chance to win a good prize or even steal the jackpot. Our genuine qualifications was being honeymooners. Forsyth kidded around before he announced Barbara and me were among the audience and he asked the rest of the mob if they wanted to see us? So after a big cheer we were on stage.

The game picked was knocking down some wooden bottles and while we were messing around I had a little rehearsal and tumbled I couldn't do it. But when the real thing came I did the trick first go. Just shows what a ham I am. I suppose it was the challenge of not losing that did it. Anyway, the buzzer goes for us to challenge for the jackpot, which was up to £800 (it increases by £100 each week when contestants fail). You had to bounce a ball on three drums and Barbara had to catch three balls in a container at the other end.

So help me, we got two balls home, had a third bounce in and out of the container, and came the closest of all the challengers. In the end they abandoned the game and bunged the prize to charity. When the same game made a come-back a few years later nobody could master it.

I'd soon had enough of laying around—though the car game was still going pretty well—and having spent money on the wedding, honeymoon, and house I was itching to fight and cop a few quid. A fighter's time is short and I figured to earn while I could. For a wonderful bit of glory the Boxing Writers' Club gave me the Best Young Boxer of the Year 1958 award. I was tickled pink.

I was back in the old routine training and Sam Burns said he'd dug up an opponent called Michel Diouf. My first reaction was saying they could keep him. I knew Diouf, black as the ace of spades from Senegal somewhere, had given Martin Hansen a right drubbing in his own backyard in Denmark. Hansen had fought out of Liverpool for a long time and I reckoned him a good man. Besides, I thought, what do I want to be messing around with Diouf for, with everything to lose and nothing much to gain? But opponents ain't easy to come by. So we signed. I was never happy about the match.

I went away to train, at Bournemouth, for the first time, which wasn't a bad idea to get away from being a newly-wed. I grabbed an old banger from the car lot (the good cars were left for sale) and with a Canadian champion, Burke Emery (a handy fighter), Johnny Berry, and Tom Ryder we motored down to set up camp.

The fight was going to kick off at Wembley for the 1959 New Year. But within a week of training, despite headguards and pillow-size gloves, my eye was grazed again.

It was a slight nick of the scar I'd got against Webb. It was enough to make me want to pack up. But Burns came to Bournemouth and, as we still had a few days to go before the fight, we figured it would heal O.K. At the time money was influencing me more than anything and, in any event, though I knew Diouf was awkward, I never figured I'd lose to him. Even with a dodgy eyebrow I still thought I'd probably be able to catch up with him early on.

It turned out to be my most stupid mistake. I was to blame for taking the fight. Burns was taken ill just before the fight, which seemed another jinx on the whole thing. The fight had only just begun, and I'd tumbled Diouf was all arms and head, when my eyebrow was ripped open. His head was like a coconut. I was right choked. I'd even lost a bit of spirit. But I don't think the crowd can say I didn't have a go. Although the referee came over to my corner three times, which is enough to dispirit anybody, I still kept plugging away.

But it was one of those fights where nothing would go right. Diouf got gamer because he could see the state of my eye and after the fifth Ryder called the referee over and retired me. All my fighting ego had gone. It wasn't that Diouf was anything great, because Phil Edwards and John McCormack licked him later, but because I wondered how long I could go on getting cut.

The Press began writing me off. 'It looks as though his career might be finished before it had begun', they said. It was a rotten night. And Willie Pastrano kept me company. He'd been well outboxed by Joe Erskine on the same bill. That's show business!

This crisis called for a conference, and considering I'd given my skin ten weeks to heal between the Webb and Diouf fights, I was worried.

So I booked a bed at the London Clinic, we got Mr. Percy Jayes, the top plastic surgeon, to do some sewing. They prepared me like I was expecting a baby, or something, with no grub and lights out the night before the operation. When I knew the cost I was frightened to ask for a headache tablet in case the bill became too strong. They cleaned me up, put me in the usual operation gear, and a nurse jabbed me with what I called a soppy needle.

I was supposed to be drowsy, but when they wheeled me away—at the time I was fit enough to fight without notice—I was pleading with the surgeon's 'seconds' that I was still feeling wide awake.

But they found a needle right up my alley. I went out like a kipper. And then they played noughts and crosses with knives on my face.

When I came round, feeling like death warmed up, Barbara was sitting at the bedside saying she was all embarrassed because I'd been chatting away in my sleep and calling the nurses 'Darling'. I never did tell her I wasn't asleep! I had bruises around the eyes and felt worse than being punched up in a fifteen-rounder. I looked like the invisible man bound in bandages, and when they put smaller patches on me I was ready for the get-away. I'm a great boy for rushing home.

I couldn't resist a little peep at the new face. It was the feeling a bank robber must have when he's had a face-lift to dodge the law. I could see the black dots of maybe thirty-odd stitches where the skin had been transplanted. It was a marvellous job, as though the surgeon had done it with a sewing-machine.

It cost me about £180—but it saved my career. It was money well spent.

But for three months I had to take it easy, massaging the skin and making sure I didn't bump into anything. But I always kept in fair shape and finally I got the O.K. to fight again.

Naturally, I was a bit careful and even scared when I first sparred in the gym, and wrapped my head up like an Arab.

But within no time I felt more confident and I signed to fight André Davier, of France, at Streatham Ice Rink. The whisperers in the fight game were saying I was finished. I was determined to get back at the top. Six months earlier I'd been a bit of a hero. Now they were saying I should quit. Gerald Walter, in the *News Chronicle*, wrote: 'I advise Downes to quit the ring now', and went on: 'The vital spark which is in all champions must die out some time, and no amount of wishful thinking or blinding oneself to stark realities will ever alter that fact.'

I've always got mad when I read that fighters should quit while they're still young. One defeat and one cut eye, at twenty-two, was not enough to make me pack up. Freddie Mills had a losing string and Don Cockell was stopped long before they wound up battling for world titles. Why pick on me? I ain't saying we fighters are professors, but give us a little bit of savvy. I would know when enough is enough. Nobody would have to remind me. But I wasn't going to be pushed out of business because of a drop of blood.

Anyway, it was a boiling hot night at Streatham, despite being an ice rink, and Davier ducked and dived and fought like a crab. After the lay-off, even discounting the eye troubles, he wasn't the kind of opponent who would flatter me. We flailed away like a couple of windmills and though ringsiders said I was cautious and probably worrying about the eyebrows I'd honestly forgotten that problem.

It was how to bump-off this French geezer that bothered me. I was short of practice and wasn't putting the punches together so easily. Then, in the fifth, my eyebrow started leaking. What a lousy feeling. This time I got mad and belted into Davier, who kept tumbling into the ropes half appealing to the referee to step in.

In the seventh I'd stuck in enough punches to stop him. Then I rushed back to the dressing-room to examine the latest injury—and have never felt so pleased! The cut was away from the new skin. The operation had survived the test, but the old skin (a bit jealous of the wash-'n'-brush-up they'd given the scarred stuff) had cut. I was back in hospital again, but it was only a fleeting visit to Moorfields for a couple of stitches.

I didn't expect a flattering Press, but thought they were a bit harsh and hadn't considered the lay-off. But I'd had the good and couldn't grumble when I got the bad. But even with this meaningless fight the *Daily Express* headlined it right across the back page—so I was still making some impact.

There was a plan for me to go to New York and fight Ralph (Tiger) Jones, who had beaten Sugar Ray, which would have steamed-up a match with Robinson if I'd won. But I kept in protective custody, as you might say. The face wasn't feeling all that clever and we decided to stay home and concentrate on defending the British title.

John McCormack, they call him 'Cowboy' because he's got bandy legs, was nominated by the Board of Control to meet me because he'd won twenty-three of twenty-four fights. Within no time we were blasting away at each other in the Press. He'd shot his mouth off about what he'd do to me and, I admit, I got the dead needle for the fight. It was probably the first time I'd ever got really worked-up for a fight. Usually I treat an opponent like another guy who has to get a living, but I regarded McCormack as somebody I wanted to belt good and proper.

Maybe I'd stood for the printed chit-chat, but, whatever it was, it worked. We were a couple of angry young men. I'd have had the needle with McCormack without him saying anything. Being a southpaw was enough. I hated 'em. And McCormack was as awkward as any of them and could punch hard.

Down at the gym Tom Ryder tried a good gimmick to stop my stance from spreading by tying my legs together with elastic. There's more to training than just swapping punches or hitting a punchball. Although I'd lost to Tiger, Cross, and Diouf because of cuts, I was still convinced I'd chop the Cowboy down.

At the weigh-in we refused to shake hands—and that wasn't a gimmick. I had nothing but contempt for him. I was sick of the chat and wanted to get on with the fight. I might even have been a bit edgy. When I left the scales a fellah starts chatting away in some brogue that could have been English, Yiddish,

Russian, or Rubbish, for all I knew, and I thought he might have been some nutty Scot who'd come to London to cheer McCormack. Before I could answer I realized the poor fellah was my best fan! His name is Bob Patterson, who'd kept writing to me from Newcastle, and he'd sent 7 lb. of coal for luck. For every fight Patterson would manage to sit up all night on a train from Newcastle to watch me fight and then go back overnight. I often wonder if I deserved such a fan. Anyway, we took Patterson out to lunch before the fight, gave him a ticket, and I still get dozens of letters, Christmas cards, and regularly cop my piece of coal for luck.

It turned out the coal was a bock—a jinx. When I shaped up to McCormack I started falling over his feet from the start. I went over three times. He was too tall to reach comfortably to the head with a punch, so I had to start whipping punches to the body to start bending him over. He was pretty easy to catch downstairs. Before we went into the ring McCormack was about 11–10 favourite, but after he'd been up and down more times than Tower Bridge I was 7–2 to win.

Whenever I moved in—which was all the time, because he was only interested in moving backwards—I fell into his lanky right arm and, to be generous, I would have given McCormack the first round. But that's all. All together I put him down *ten* times—yes, *ten*—for a total of sixty-five seconds, *yet lost my title!*

Only once, in the fourth, did I manage to drop him with a punch on the chin. The rest were all up the belly. Every time I looked at McCormack he'd start looking at the referee, Ike Powell, from Wales. I belted him some smashing punches to the body and, since I was closer than the referee, take my word for it they were not low. But I did get warned later for a low punch, though I don't think it could have hurt McCormack. 'They are borderline,' said the ref.

But as a fight it was a farce. He'd fold up with the first sign of a body punch and with the referee pulling me off and him squirming and face-pulling I still don't know how I kept my temper. What kind of championship fight was this? It stunk. I could have got a better fight at a fairground booth.

Yet after the seventh, with the referee in a right state and counting over McCormack more times than a wrestling referee, I told Sam Burns in the corner to call Powell over and protest. 'I'm bound to get disqualified if this geezer keeps this up,' I said to Burns. 'He should get disqualified for falling over without being hit. Let's tell the ref.'

Why should I stop hitting him up the belly because he didn't like it? But before we could do anything about it the bell had gone for the eighth round. As far as I was concerned the fight had become a stupid bore. The crowd were entitled to their money back. In the eighth he did try to come forward—and fell on his face. When he got up I chased him all around the ring and as I started a punch to the body McCormack bounced at me from the ropes and the punch landed at about the top of his shorts. I suppose you could say it was borderline. But there was absolutely no power in it. In any case, I can't punch a hole in a pound of butter.

Down he went again—it got to a state when I didn't recognize him standing up!—but referee Powell, a little man, flung his arms around my waist and absolutely manhandled me away. *I was disqualified!*

I got out of the ring too disgusted to talk and when I stop talking you can bet it's serious. McCormack was hauled off the floor, well beaten, bleeding from the nose, yet champion. Even his manager refused to get into the ring when Viscount Scarsdale put the Lonsdale Belt around McCormack's waist. And he never even took the Belt home. I think that summed up how even he must have been embarrassed. He was the first Scot to become 11 st. 6 lb. champion since Alex Ireland in 1928—who also won by a foul! While all the shindig was going on, Solomons was on the ring apron trying to settle a return there and then. What he didn't know was that I was not interested in a return. I didn't even want revenge.

If a man could win a British championship clutching his belly he could keep it. I reckoned it made a mockery of boxing. All right, if they thought my punch was low, punish me—but don't give him the title. And then to top it up, the Board of Control fined me £100 for throwing what the referee thought was a low blow. I thought that was adding insult to injury. The first time I'd ever been disqualified, amateur or pro, and they hit me hard. I was at least hoping to get some moral 'victory' by not being fined.

I still think the fight and the fine was a diabolical liberty. It knocked all the pride out of winning a championship. I couldn't care less—and my opinion still hasn't changed. They can keep their titles.

Sam Burns signed up the return, but I was so choked, Barbara—who, by the way, had had our first baby, Wendy, only a month before—reckoned I should get away from it all. So I went to Spain with a couple of mates—and still said they could forget all about another championship fight. And, truthfully, I meant it.

While I held the title for a year I began to feel the Board of Control were taking over my management. They laid down orders and my manager became a bit of a go-between. It might suit them but it didn't suit me.

No matter how much Burns and Astaire pressed, I still didn't want the return. The consolation, at the time, was baby Wendy. Her arrival surprised me almost as much as the fight referee.

While I was training for McCormack, Barbara woke me up in the night and complained she felt pains. The baby was not expected for another fortnight and I couldn't believe these rules could be broken. I thought Barbara was flapping a bit. Anyway, she forced me to drive her down to the local hospital— well named, being off Honey Pot Lane—and I'm half apologizing to the Sister because I think Barbara has shown us both up. I'm right embarrassed knowing I'll go back and fetch her out the next day.

'You don't understand these things. You go home,' said the Sister. O.K., so I wasn't arguing. But I still felt a right chump. But the joke was on me. When I went back next day Barbara had Wendy like it was having a hot dinner. I was a proud dad.

While I was in Spain I must have cooled down, because when they kept saying public opinion demanded a return with McCormack I figured I'd have to take it, otherwise they might even think I was scared of the geezer! But it burned me up that I was only offered £1,500 as challenger, while I presumed he copped more for being a so-called champion. Without me in the other corner I didn't reckon McCormack could draw his breath at the box-office in London. How comes I was paying out part of my end to him? This is the way of the boxing game. It has always narked me. But even I realized I couldn't afford to go on being stubborn—and agreed to fight . . . forty-seven days after the fiasco.

The Press had argued about a no-foul rule, they called McCormack 'the sit-down champion', and so much controversy was going on that the return was bound to be a seller at Wembley. If I was a fan I wouldn't have gone round the corner to see it for nothing. But it was another sell-out!

We got the publicity going asking for Rocky Marciano to be the referee, though nobody could seriously have thought the Board of Control would allow it. But I was really pleased when they appointed Andrew Smyth, of Belfast, an amateur but a great ref—the best. I knew he wouldn't panic about blood or low blows.

The fight, more or less, turned out the way I'd expected, except it was much harder and bloodier, and me and McCormack finished up mates! I figured he'd come out throwing punches early on to prove he wanted to have a go. I was right. So for the first couple of rounds I stood off, kept the hands a bit higher, and let McCormack punch away. He could hit pretty good, but I wasn't bothered. 'Go on, me son,' I was thinking. 'You won't be able to keep that up for long. Then you'll get some back. You will enjoy yourself.'

I never threw a single body punch in the first round. I wanted to knock him out on the chin—and almost came unstuck. Plans are not much good when cuts come and you've got to do something desperate. Thank God in the second round his nose bled and he had a bit of a graze over the eye. At first I thought the blood on his face might have come from mine! But I was looking like a good 'un.

In the fourth I started pressuring and had him rolling around the ring a bit and I figured he'd already shot his bolt.

He'd been a lot gamer than the first time, but when he'd seen his punches made no difference he wasn't looking so brave. I started to go in style, not a blemish on my face, and fists firing away. Then suddenly, in a matter of seconds, my left eye started to swell and was closed. I can't recall how it happened, but we probably bumped heads. This turnabout gave McCormack some new life and for a while he was whacking a few fair right-handers at me. I stumbled a couple of times because I couldn't see the punches coming.

In the fifth I'd made up my mind to switch to the body and start cutting him down. But, bang, I got the most choice cut on my nose that you've ever seen. It was V-shaped and flapping about. The blood poured down over my lips. Oh, blimey, the championship looked like being gone for good! I'd never had the slightest bother with my nose, the old hooter, until this fight. It wound up getting more publicity than Schnozzle Durante's.

I got back to the corner and told the seconds: 'Stop this cut any way you have to. I can lick this geezer with one eye.' By the looks on their faces I was in dead trouble. But Ryder did a good job stemming the blood and referee Smyth, bless him, was as good as gold. He didn't keep pestering in the corner to give the other guy even more confidence. He took one look and left the decision to the seconds. He knew there was a lot at stake and I'd ended the round belting McCormack all over the place.

I went out for the seventh feeling that if I couldn't win the fight I'd probably forget all about the game. I was right mad with him, myself, and everything else. I pinned McCormack on the ropes and must have landed two dozen punches and stuck him down for a nine count. Although McCormack was sinking, he'd look up at me and the sight of the blood flowing gave him heart to get up. So I knocked him over again.

The bell went and I felt I couldn't expect the referee to let me go on much longer, even though I was winning so easily. I'm always grateful that Smyth had the courage to let me go on and win. It would have been another mockery if I'd been stopped. So I made no mistake in the eighth. I chased

McCormack to put him down three times for a nine-count and, though I couldn't keep him down, he was so exhausted and punched-out he dropped over the top rope. I felt like one of the wrestlers you see wanting to tip the other guy out of the ring. While the ref was counting, I half turned my face away to somehow stop reminding him how bad I looked.

But Mr. Smyth signalled the fight was over, and I was the champ . . . at a price. I'd regained the title in a world-record number of days and been the first British middle-weight to get the title back since Pat O'Keefe in 1914.

I got the Lonsdale Belt back, I'd regained my pride, and had the bloodiest fight of my career, for less money than I've earned in easier fights since. The Press said: 'A Triumph of Guts', 'Demon Downes', 'What a Fight!'

In the dressing-room I was so excited and mobbed by the family and what-not that I'd forgotten my golden rule about never having stitches in the dressing-room. A doctor put some in my nose and later it came up in a lump and made me look like a clown. McCormack came to see me and all the pre-fight hate had gone. 'You're the gamest guy I know,' he said, and we both looked into a mirror and laughed: 'Is it all worth it?' We both looked like a film with an 'H' certificate.

Then we shared a cup of tea and chatted. With all the tough talk around I think John—he was my mate now—was a bit embarrassed and walked out. I never dreamed that I'd later go to Scotland and second him! My nagging in the corner helped him to outpoint a good American, George Benton. And old Archie Moore was there to see it. It's a funny game, the fight game. I had 'em in stitches going back to hospital. . . .

Out-roughing an American

WHEN I went through the front door at the London Clinic —it was a toss-up at the time who was the best customer, me or Elizabeth Taylor—they started sharpening up the sewing needles. My nose, the old hooter, wanted some upholstering, a bit more meat on it. It had split open like the back of an envelope and the after-fight patching up had only screwed it up even worse. So I had to wait until it straightened itself out before Mr. Jayes would consider his expert repairing.

It was a G.P. doctor, Bill Kelsey, who practises in Islington, London, and comes around a lot to the fights, who first convinced me it was better to have plastic stitching. Doc Kelsey's wisdom has helped many a fighter. So he came with me to Boston when I fought Paul Pender and turned our bedroom into an impromptu operating theatre—with me, of course, the patient!

I owe a great deal to men like Kelsey and Jayes. And, later, Mr. Arthur Dickson Wright, another master surgeon, did a bit of homework on me. I'm proud to say both still come to watch me fight. I try to make sure they are there. Percy Jayes was a right-hand man of the late Archibald McIndoe at East Grinstead Hospital, where they 'repaired' the servicemen, mostly R.A.F., whose faces had been disfigured. So performing on me was child's stuff. What great men, the surgeon and patients. Mr. Jayes must have seen sights at the guinea-pig hospital that would make my face look a pin-up by comparison. Yes, great men. I can't put into words how much respect I have for them.

Anway, they gave me the wash-'n'-brush-up, diet and jabs,

and Mr. Jayes' 'job' was marvellous. It looked as though he'd sewn-up with invisible needles. I was about a hundred-guinea pig, but it was worth every penny. The old hooter was ready for blows and blowing again. The re-mould suited me fine.

Before the stitches healed I was restless, as usual, and rushing home again. I don't really know why, because I knew I couldn't fight for about three months. Being out of the ring was the real aggravation. From November 1959 to March 1960 I was chiefly fiddling around the car sites making a crust and keeping fit with road-work. I always kept in trim running around Hampstead Heath. I never spared myself. Running was important to me to maintain stamina and keep the lungs and legs strong.

To keep future hospital costs down I sent to the States for a special headguard for sparring. It cost me £40 to have made. It had a leather-covered metal bar protecting the nose. I looked like a soldier geared-up for the Battle of Hastings. It was cumbersome, but necessary.

Having survived the early sparring sessions, I felt pretty good, despite the rest. Perhaps I was feeling fresher. But getting a fight wasn't so easy. Solomons had planned his next show, and there wasn't room for me, so I told Sam Burns to ask Harry Levene to fix-up a fight.

I hadn't fought on a Levene promotion and Burns said I wouldn't be too popular with Solomons if I changed boats mid-stream. In fact, my managers told me that Solomons had said he would never offer me a fight again if I fought for Levene. That was a chance I had to take. I was too anxious to get cracking again to concern myself with politics. I figured that if I couldn't get fixed up on the next Solomons show, supposing Levene scrubbed me out because I'd never offered to fight for him? I'd be out of business. Other champions had fought for both promoters, so why not me? This business of the pro-moters playing Cowboys and Indians and keeping their own circle of fighters is ridiculous. I've earned from both camps.

It was my decision—or demand, if you like—that Burns did business with Levene. It's funny how the boxing game in Britain centres around Solomons and Levene, whose feud is no joke. A lot of people ask me if their rivalry is just a stunt. No kidding, it's the nearest thing to war! They are different personalities, both with a long background in boxing.

Jack, who was matchmaker in pre-war days for Sydney Hulls (father of the *Daily Express* boxing writer) at Harringay Arena, and promoter at the Devonshire Club in London's East End, is a jovial man, with a flair for showmanship, and a smart business brain. He also, I reckon, revels a bit too much in the glory he gets from being a big promoter. He was also once chairman of the Southern Area council of the Boxing Board of Control before they brought in non-financially interested councils. So, you can imagine, Solomons had sway.

When Harringay closed down, having to share Wembley with Levene didn't exactly help the rivalry. It got even more bitter. Each wants to be bigger and better than the other. Each would 'favour' certain fighters in the hope of keeping their loyalty. Neither fancies building up a fighter to benefit the other. So whether a manager likes it or not—unless he happens to handle an oustanding fighter—he's bound to give loyalty to one or the other. The only time both promoters are on merit is when a championship fight cannot be signed because the respective managers are haggling over purse-money and the Board of Control accept sealed bids for the fight The highest bidder wins.

Levene, who keeps his age a secret—but he'll still recognize the scenery when he's sixty!—is a successful manager who turned promotor about twelve years ago. He'd managed champions Jock McAvoy, Larry Gains, Dave Crowley, and you can bet he'll never finish a conversation without mentioning either Gains or McAvoy. To Harry they're still the greatest. He must have been a real cute manager. He's a smart dresser, a bachelor, who lives in Park Lane, and whose bark is worse than his bite. When Harry starts yelling you can hear it from his office all over Soho. Usually the argument is about money— because he worries about it. Perhaps a bit too much. Me and ole Harry have something in common. Our noses don't 'arf give the cartoonists a chance to get a giggle.

Solomons and Levene both put their own money up, at a fair risk, to promote. It's an aggravating living, though all promoters like limelight. And when they take a hammering at the box-office it takes a long time to make a come-back. Boxing has a lot to thank them for. But I reckon they take themselves too seriously. Boxing would survive without either of them—and that goes for Terry Downes, too. But while their feud goes on—and, remember, they never exchange words or even meet face-to-face—boxers get more money. In some ways the 'war' has been good for competition. One man getting his own way doesn't arf keep the purses down.

Anyway, while Burns was dwelling on doing business with Levene, Dave Rent, the heavy-weight from Liverpool who tried his luck in America, withdrew from a Levene show. He was stuck for a replacement and, by luck, approached us. It couldn't have been at a better time. I told Sam to stick out for good money but grab the job. I needed it, and to hell with the consequences. Also on Levene's bill were Americans Virgil Akins, former world champ, and Del Flanagan. It turned out to be a dreary bill.

They put me in with a Belgian, Carlos Vanneste, who'd won his ten fights the previous year. For my part he could have been another Soho waiter. The only reason he lasted four rounds was because I couldn't get an earlier good whack at him. I was pleased with the way I'd fought, even allowing for the opposition, and the ole hooter came out without a blemish. They paid me £2,000 for that little job, the same as I'd got for the war with Spider Webb. So where had this Harry Levene been all my life? This was handy money. There was no showing-off or spouting in the dressing-room from me after this fight. I'd started getting a little more knowledge in the bonce. I'd learned my lesson being pitched in with Webb and, because of it, I'd spent the months out of the ring. Really it was a blessing in disguise. Promoters could forget all about bunging me in against top Yanks again until I was good and ready. I'd learn the trade against home boys or Continentals. That was for sure.

On hand at Wembley was Mickey Duff, who's 'in' more

things than a moth, and it was a toss-up whose nose was the tastiest—mine, his, or Levene's. We'd make a good win treble. I tell Mickey my nose has fought for the championship, so what is his excuse?

Mickey's real name is Morris Praegar. He got the ring moniker from a James Cagney film called *Cash and Carry*. He was born in Poland, came to London as a kid, and is now as much of a Londoner as me. He knows boxing as good as anybody, and better than most. Somebody should write a book about Duff, because he's a real character.

Anyway, Mickey of the million words offered me a fight at Liverpool Stadium where he promoted. Liverpool was always a fight-crazy town and they used to idolize fighters like Nel Tarleton, Ernie Roderick, and McAteer before the Beatles came on the scene. Apart from the money—which came first! —I fancied performing at the Stadium, which is perfect for boxing. They call it the Graveyard of Champions—because the original Stadium was built on a graveyard—and it proved to be a grave joint for me.

I hadn't fought outside London for three years. The out-of-town experience was good. Duff dug up a Yank called Orlando Di Pietro, a white cruiser-weight from Arcadia, California. He wasn't a pushover, because he'd taken Joey Giambra—whom I always reckoned a class man—to a disputed decision at Long Beach. He'd won twenty-six of thirty-six fights, thirteen by k.o., and was first to beat Don Fullmer. He reckoned he'd been sidestepped in the States because he was a good spoiler. He wasn't kidding.

I spotted a few pounds to Di Pietro, who was nearly 6 ft. and could grab like a crab. He banged his head into me like a battering-ram. The referee, Fred Hampson, kept warning Di Pietro to keep his head up. He even issued a final warning— but it came too late. In the third he cracked his nut into my nose and I was back in the bleeding business again. The cut was deep and vertical but away from the horizontal scar I'd got from McCormack. The new nose had stood the test but the old one was going soft.

I was so mad I banged away at Di Pietro and he sat on one

knee to be counted out in the fourth round. He'd quit. The crowd booed him and somebody threw an apple-core at Di Pietro to help him on his way up the aisle. When he got back to the dressing-room they asked the American why he didn't get up. 'What was the use?' he said. 'I'd have only got knocked down again.' He wasn't kidding, either. Having done the damage, he'd nicely ducked out before I could really give him a going-over

In my dressing-room I made quips about the nose looking like a crossword puzzle—but I was broken-hearted. We went, immediately, to Liverpool Northern Hospital to find Mr. Geoffrey Osborne, a noted surgeon. I wasn't going to settle for any second-rater. The ole nose deserved the best service, even though I still couldn't understand why I should cut so easily. Nobody has ever seen any other fighter get more ridiculous cuts on their nose. I still can't fathom out why— except I shouldn't get hit so much.

We tried to keep the visit to hospital quiet, but you can't hide your face, and the newspapers soon got the story. Mr. Osborne decided to dash across town, at midnight, with me for a further chat with another surgeon at the Southern Hospital.

The next thing I know I'm back in a hospital bed, screens around me, and feeling right fed-up. They'd done another good job sewing up the hooter, but an operation directly after a fight ain't too healthy. I admit I have never felt so low. This was the closest I'd ever come to retirement. I kept think-ing that all the years of training and preparing meant nothing if I was going to get cut-up with every fight. I didn't want to discuss anything with Tom Ryder or Sam Burns who'd both been waiting and wandering around the hospital ward. Nothing they could say could cheer me up. Downes and all his chat had nothing to say. I was too choked-up.

Next morning I awoke in a public ward, feeling like death warmed up, with screens around me. But the moment I could open my eyes, even though I felt dizzy and sick to the heart, I couldn't wait to rush home. The doctors weren't too pleased with the idea, but they couldn't stop me. I almost wobbled to catch the train to Euston, which arrived at 5.56 on Platform 13—so you can imagine my luck.

Reporters were there, and photographers had a ball getting photos of the ole hooter all plastered up. For two pins I'd have turned the fighting game up there and then. But I loved the fuss and braved it out. On the platform I told Harry Carpenter, who I knew was digging hard for a good story, that I'd be fighting again within six weeks. Having said that, I wasn't going to back down. I like to think I'm a man of my word. Besides, I'd spent over £400 getting my face repaired. I was entitled to nick my money back.

The old-iron headguard started being worn again and after Burns and Astaire had encouraged me I was matched (for Harry Levene again) at Belle Vue, Manchester. Richard Bouchez, a Belgian, was nicely hand-picked. I wasn't standing for anyone too murderous, because I was getting to the stage where I was wondering where I would be cut next. Yet I can't honestly say I ever worried. That might or might not be a silly thing to admit, but that's the way I am. What's the use of worrying? Bouchez looked like a hat-rack and I had no trouble hanging a few punches on his chin. I figured if I kept tearing in and hitting him I was less likely to get hit back. It worked. I did a good job and Bouchez went out like a good 'un in two rounds.

Although Bouchez hardly tested the nose I'd tossed away the mask in training and let the sparring-partners have a real go at me. I was satisfied that plastic surgery had saved me. But I needed a boost. So we signed to defend the middle-weight title against Phil Edwards—for £5,000. That's what I called a pay-day. And since I always figured to beat Edwards, though I knew it would have to be another hard fight, it was handy being able to take the Lonsdale Belt home for keeps.

Winning the title and defending it twice entitles a champion to keep the Belt—and he gets a £1-a-week pension at fifty. I hope the Board of Control are still in business when my pay-out is due!

Levene was well pleased signing me for a title fight and I'd secretly been building up strength with weight-lifting instuction from Ed Bolton, a specialist, after another of my doctor chums, Chris Woodard, had advised it. I often went to Doc Chris for a check-up after fights. I never left anything to chance. Fitness is my business. Some of the diehard trainers are against weight-lifting because they reckon it tightens up a boxer. Too many muscles cause slowness. But I contend that boxing training has not moved enough with the times. We're still bashing away at the same routines—skip, spar, and punch at speed-balls— while athletes are improving their techniques all the time. Trouble is, boxing doesn't provide enough brainy trainers.

My weight-lifting routine was designed solely to produce a bit more snap in my punching. I wasn't hitting hard enough to reach world class—and I knew it. A bit of extra strength in the clinches also comes in handy. At least I was willing to have a go.

I trained as hard as I could for Edwards, because the challenge of losing the title was more than I could bear. I'd had enough with the two punch-ups with McCormack and wasn't going to go through that annoyance again.

In the two years that Edwards and me had first fought he'd stayed undefeated. Phil's manager, Benny Jacobs, was a smart manœuvrer and kept him pegging away. Benny was always sure Edwards could beat me. It seemed a shame to disappoint him.

Somebody came up with a brainwave to bring champion Paul Pender, of Boston, over to watch the fight. Pender had twice beaten Sugar Ray Robinson—the first man to lick Sugar twice—for the world title. He'd won it fair and square, which is why I always got mad when some critics called him a half-champion because Gene Fullmer was recognized by the then National Boxing Association of America. Pender won the title in rightful succession—and was undisputed champ. I wouldn't back down on that one. The N.B.A. titles were a joke.

I think Pender was probably persuaded to come to London more to push the publicity for the show than to fight me. He was a former fireman from Brookline, Boston, and when I was introduced for the first time I reckoned my nose, alongside his, looked a treat. Pender's hooter was bent like a big dipper at Battersea Fun Fair. If this had happened to a supposedly classic defensive boxer, God help me, I'd settle for being a defenceless fighter.

With Pender was his manager, Johnny Buckley, an old-timer who had managed Jack Sharkey to the world heavyweight championship. He must have known more strokes than Joe Davis. A year later little old Buckley was writing letters to my managers telling them how I could beat Pender! He and Pender had a bust-up and Buckley wanted me to take it out on him. But that was none of my business.

Just to explain the difference between the American and British fight mob, Buckley was also charged with attacking his own son-in-law, so you can see he was a game old guy. Mind you, he had a gun in his hand at the time.

Paying his own expenses for the trip to London with Pender was John Cronin, a Boston lawyer who had served with the F.B.I. He later replaced Buckley as adviser. Pender had a lot to thank Cronin for. He was the only fighter I knew who got his TV rake-off in America from the sponsors Gillette Razor Co., paid on a spread-over basis to ease tax problems. He should never be skint.

Cronin had read in the Massachusetts Press that Pender, whom he'd never met, was having a battle with the local commission. He volunteered to fight Pender's case—for free. Cronin won and became interested in the fight game. But he has not bothered to involve himself with fighters since Pender retired. Cronin comes to Britain frequently, and seldom misses a big fight in the States.

If I went back to the big-time in America, Cronin could work for me—especially if it was for free!

Fighting Edwards again was the perfect chance, I reckoned, to convince Pender I was ready for him without being too good for my own good. I knew Edwards was bound to stay on his feet. I doubt if Pender would have knocked him over. After sixty-four fights the 'Taffy' was tough and knew the ropes.

In some ways I'd have done Phil a favour being able to knock him out, because I dished out such a hammering that he took more stick than is healthy for another twelve rounds— one round shorter than before. His manager did Phil a bigger favour retiring him.

For twelve rounds we belted away at each other, but he

couldn't whack hard enough to hurt me. I kept up such a pace that he finally folded up exhausted, with his face in a right state. The only time Edwards really looked like going down was when I caught him a right-hander just as the bell sounded after the tenth. The punch (honest!) was on its way before the bell, but Benny Jacobs, as a good manager should, blamed this for the defeat.

Take it from me, the punch didn't make the slightest difference. Edwards was just my handwriting. He could beat boys who beat me, but he could never handle me. But he had my admiration. He went out like a real game fighter should. Peter Wilson reported: 'Tearaway Terry! . . . Edwards had gradually been unfleshed, hammered and beaten and tossed from one set of ropes to another. He was a slack-legged squinting marionette, sagging and lurching helplessly.'

Like I said—he was in a right state. That's my way of describing it. Harry Carpenter wrote: 'Edwards's final moments in this cruel battle were painful to watch, painful to record.'

At the ringside Pender told somebody I'd make a good opponent for a heavy-weight! It didn't sound as though he was too keen about fighting me. In the dressing-room I looked in the mirror and when they cleaned me up proudly discovered my face was practically unmarked—but I had a painful blister on my foot and a dozen little cuts on my head! We must have been banging away in the clinches like billygoats.

After I'd whooped it up in the ring getting my Lonsdale Belt, giving Barbara a kiss—that was a photo for the front pages—and blowing out kisses to the crowd, Mr. Arthur Dickson Wright came to congratulate me. I think he had a soft spot for me because I'd been such a good client to the medical profession and because my face reminded him of his car radiator grill—bashed in with an accident. Dickson Wright, who originally came from Dublin, is a brilliant surgeon, one of the country's leading cancer specialists, does terrific work for Cancer Research Funds, and is one of the best after-dinner speakers I've ever heard. He's such an entertainer they say he ought to have a toastmaster to attend his operations.

I only hope that Dickson Wright is knighted soon. I think it's scandalous that a man like him is passed over. Yet some geezer who plays third bassoon in a symphony band gets honoured and cricketers knighted. It don't make sense to me.

Whenever I meet Dickson Wright we usually have a wise-cracking match. When he came into the dressing-room I said: 'Come on, guv'nor, don't lay about doing nothing. Get the tools out and start stitching.' I was only kidding. But, calling the bluff, he led me out of Wembley, with Barbara and Lonsdale Belt (I'll put the missus top of the bill for a change), supporters and all, and drove to St. Mary's Hospital, Paddington.

He opened up a surgery, switched on the arc-lights, and enjoyed himself sewing up my head cuts. That'll teach me to talk. But Terry Downes only has the best hands on him.

So from the winter months of depression I'd recovered and was bang on top of the world again. Now my managers had to bang away to get me a world-title fight. This is the time when you can sort the good manager from the fraud. Anyone with a reasonable knowledge of the fight game can manage a boy around the halls of Britain where the Board of Control virtually do the championship-fight matching.

But moving into the American league is a different job. You can soon sort the men from the boys. Pender had gone home and helped boost my claims—which is more than I could say, at the time, for our Boxing Board.

So, with Barbara's permission, I decided to holiday with the boys. And, like the nut I am, I had to be cheering boxing. It was Olympic year in Rome, and Danny O'Brien, who was as Cockney as they come, and kicked around with us in Paddington, was representing Ireland. So with cousin Cyril, Tom Ryder, and Pat Carey, a pal of Danny's, we motored through France, making a holiday of it, and on to Rome.

I'd taken my boxing kit in the car solely for the purpose of having a few rounds with any of the British boys if they wanted a livener. I happen to be enthusiastic and love cheering the boys on, but I hadn't reckoned on the bombastic A.B.A. officials.

We motored round, following 'Olympiad Village' signs, and it took us three days to realize that the Italian wags enjoyed turning the signs round just for a giggle. Anyway, we eventually found the team village, but, naturally, couldn't get in. So we went down to a local hat-shop, armed ourselves with a panama apiece, slung our coats on arms to pretend they were team blazers—and bowled past the Italian guards. 'British team', I'd say, and looking at my face he knew I wasn't one of the ping-pong players. We chatted away with Dave Thomas, the heavy-weight who came from Paddington and often sparred with me, Dick McTaggart, the Scot who won every amateur title, Bob Kelsey, of London, and, of course, our mate Danny.

I fancied going with the British team to watch them work out and maybe just give them a bit of encouragement. But they turned us off the team coach going to the gym. I could understand working-to-rule and all that rubbish, but I got mad at the way the officials did it. I can't stand pumped-up officialdom. It makes me sick.

We were game enough to follow the coach in our car, then creep in the gym. You'd think I'd have better things to do, but having motored all the way from England I couldn't resist watching the boys.

But, again, I was ordered out like I had the plague. 'Whose side are you on?' I told the A.B.A. official. He must have thought I was spying for the Russians, or something, but I can tell you I was sick of the attitude. So long as I wasn't actually interfering I couldn't see the harm of giving the boys some encouragement. They weren't all strangers to me and the last thing I cared about was whether they were gonna be pro's.

The German team welcomed the cheer-up they got from Max Schmeling and the American team certainly didn't order Floyd Patterson out when he arrived in Rome on the final day.

What I didn't tell the A.B.A. was that the middle-weight champion of Great Britain was camping out in a field because he couldn't get an hotel booking. So, by fooling the team-camp guards, I spent most of the time scoffing in the team canteen

My betting shop empire – inside, in 1963

And outside, in 1966

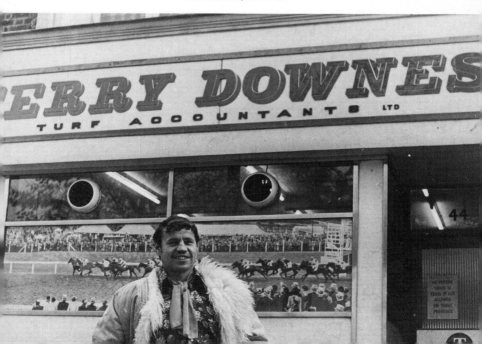

With my family in the summer of 1967. Terry Junior is on my knee, baby Richard on my wife Barbara's knee, while Paul and Wendy look on

Terry Junior lands a punch, 1967

But prefers to stay out of the ring, with brother Paul, when it's for real

In his father's footsteps – Paul has a go

Our youngest son Richard is determined not to be outdone – outside our home in 1969

and generally living it up. It was a bit of a liberty, but harmless.

But at the boxing arena, when it was often half empty in the afternoon, it was me and my mates who were the only people to give our boys a cheer. I should have thought they would have welcomed any help from home. No wonder we didn't even smell a medal—apart from the third places won by Jim Lloyd, of Liverpool, and Willie Fisher, of Scotland.

The Irish team, who welcomed us much more, didn't have any luck, and Danny was having weight trouble and had a pulled back muscle that messed up his chances. Later Danny was working for me in a betting shop. Now he is a taxi-driver— and retired from pro fighting in our stable.

Despite the aggravation, I came home ready to get back into action and I realized I can't stand still for ever. I wanted to convince myself I was ready for world class. But unless I could beat a world-rated American nobody in the States would take me seriously. Somebody had to be the fall guy. We chose Joey Giardello—who three years later became the world middle-weight champion. Giardello, a man I respected in the ring, was my important stepping-stone. It was useless trying to build up a world-title match with Pender unless I had the right win.

Harry Levene didn't mess about, he signed Giardello—but as it turned out poor ole Harry never saw the fight. He was taken seriously ill. But when the show was a sell-out I think it made Harry get better a lot quicker carrying the money to the bank.

My whack of the proceedings was £6,000, which was the best pay-day I'd had at that time. Giardello, whose real name is Carmen Tillelli, comes from Philadelphia. When he fought me Joey was thirty, and having his 109th fight in twelve years compared with my twenty-nine fights. You name 'em and Giardello had fought 'em. He lost and won against Dick Tiger in Chicago and Cleveland and later took the world title from Tiger in Atlantic City.

Joey was quite a character. In 1952 he had to win a fight twice to get the verdict. The New York Commission altered a judge's card after Giardello had outpointed Billy Graham at Madison Square Garden and reversed the decision. But when Joey appealed to the State Supreme Court the judge decided the Commission had no right to interfere. Joey officially got the verdict.

At the time of writing Giardello is still not licensed in New York State, even though he's undisputed world champion. It probably stems from the days when Giardello cracked a gas-station attendant across the nut with one of the crutches Joey happened to be using to support a broken foot. He served a sentence. Joey reckoned it was all a misunderstanding at the time, though I'll bet the guy who got the whack couldn't see the joke. But I'm glad to say Joey had lived down that blemish and became a popular champion when he was big odds against in the fight with Dick Tiger.

When Giardello arrived at London Airport, wearing a black detective-style hat, his face was so covered with ring trade-marks that I thought they'd sent a substitute for the guy whose publicity photos had been sent here. The Press called him 'Scarface', which, apparently, didn't please Giardello too much. Because he was such a good fighter and a real husky-voiced character straight out of a film, he got great publicity. The fight couldn't miss as an attraction.

With Giardello was trainer Joe Polino, another gravel-voiced geezer, as tough as nails, who knew all the angles. He also worked with Sonny Liston. Since Giardello was known in the States as a 'bleeder', Polino always had his hands full as the official cut-man in the corner. Joey's only three stoppages, spread over the twelve years against the best, had come from cuts. A few months before he fought me, Giardello had drawn with Gene Fullmer for the N.B.A. version of the world title.

Giardello and Fullmer butted each other like bulls during the fifteen rounds. It must have been blood-curdling stuff. So what-ever happened I knew I couldn't afford to mix it with Joey. Certainly he was gonna be the best butter I'd ever butted against. But when the fight came I used my 'nut' another way.

I planned to fight a moving fight. Giardello, I knew, ex-pected a walk-in fighter and he could handle them with ease.

He was loaded with class, could hit with all types of punches, and was cute. His punches hurt, too. I could understand why he'd survived those years against the best—and is still tops!

But I'd always claimed critics underrated my boxing ability. Nearly all of them tipped Giardello because I'd lost to the only other world-class Yank I'd fought. This was a make-or-break match. I didn't blame the critics going overboard for Giardello, because his training in Britain showed him to be a great workman.

It gives me pleasure to say that I beat Giardello beyond dispute. My life, it was the best I'd fought! A peak night when everything went right. I knew I'd get chopped up a bit lively if I tried mixing it, so I switched to a style few in Britain had seen from me. I boxed! I jabbed and moved, I feinted, I hooked, and whenever he wanted to slow the pace I stepped it up.

A couple of times my left hand jabbed into Giardello's face and he began arguing while the fight was going on. He reckoned I'd thumbed him. Me, trying to out-rough one of America's toughest fighters? 'You'd better get your eye out of the way, mate,' I said, and started clipping him again. He couldn't frighten me. I was in tip-top form. I'd spent a good few quid hiring sparring-partners and had Larry Baker, of America, a smart fighter, plus Johnny van Rensburg, of South Africa, and reliable 'Trunky' Berry helping me.

For ten rounds we kept up a cracking pace and gave the fans a real good fight. I enjoyed it. Because both of us looked like refugees from the emergency ward everyone expected a blood-bath. It turned out fairly clean. The crowd had a little nobble at Giardello for using his forearm, but I wasn't worried, and the Board of Control inspector in Giardello's corner insisted his seconds stop using a stimulant. I got a cut over the left eye early on in the fight, but Ryder had no trouble patching me up. Giardello was marked-up, but not enough to horrify anyone.

In the ninth he caught me a hellava good left hook and my legs quivered a bit, but I was determined to stay restrained. I'd plugged away at such a pace that Joey's legs were slowing and I went into the last round knowing that I couldn't lose.

I'd passed my test—and referee Tommy Little automatically

held up my hand. Giardello didn't complain. When he got back to the dressing-room he flopped out like a stretcher case, with his face covered in ice-packs and his hand dipped in an ice-bucket. I'd exhausted him.

The Press, though they'd tipped a loser, were full of praise with a big splash. 'Zippy Downes Wins', said the *Daily Sketch*. 'The Yank is Crushed', said the *Daily Herald*. 'Downes—Boxing Artist', said the *Daily Mirror*. I'd had my usual bit of fun when the decision was given by walking round the ring sorting out the writers who'd tipped Giardello. Next day I went to the *Evening News* offices and they were good sports publishing a photo of me hitting (well, almost) their critic Reg Gutteridge for opposing me. I often paid visits to the newspaper offices after a fight. I liked to collect their action pictures. I ain't shy about looking at my photo. I love it.

The win, as we planned, had been well publicized in America and Pender's connections started biting the bait. The transatlantic phones started buzzing, with Sam Silverman, the Boston promoter, the man who had brought Pender back into the limelight, trying to get to terms with Burns and Astaire.

You'd be amazed how involved it becomes to tie-up a world-title match. The challenger usually gets kicked around a bit, but I couldn't complain. It took three months of negotiation, with letters, cables, and phones buzzing, before we finally settled the fight for Boston on January 14, 1961. After the haggling the final agreement was actually made in a three-minute phone call from Boston to London.

There were the usual wise guys of the fight game—most of them with the seats out of their trousers—going around saying I'd never get the fight. But we made it. I had to agree to a return clause in the event of winning though this enforced signing is supposed to be illegal now. I'd have signed my life away to get the fight. The championship would be televised live, with the Boston area blacked out, and I would draw 15 per cent of the gate with a fixed guarantee from the TV rights.

Look out, America, here I come. . . .

Pender Wins by a Nose!

A WORLD-championship fight is the prize for every fighting man and when it happens he has to stuff every ounce of heart, strength, and skill into it. More than anything else, he must be mentally prepared. You've gotta be right in the nut. After whipping Giardello I reckoned to be ready.

Less than a month before the fight, when I'd knuckled down to full training, Barbara and me were hoping for the perfect Christmas present—our second kid. I was playing in a charity darts match when they came to tell me Barbara had been rushed to hospital and her condition was bad. When I arrived she had lost the baby. It's the sort of personal tragedy that I'd sooner forget. I still get choked when I think about it.

I don't mind admitting it tore my heart out at the time and must have upset me for the big fight. But it's the last thing I'd claim. I remember starting to snap at people, a bit of friction crept in with Tom Ryder, and, to cap it all, I started getting a bad muscular pain in my back.

I returned to my second home in Baltimore, taking Barbara and daughter Wendy with me. Naturally my trainer came along. Getting away from it all, with Barbara making her first trip to the States, was just the tonic she needed. Barbara fixed to stay with Sylvie in Baltimore while I went on to Boston. They made a terrific fuss of me in Baltimore. The prodigal son had returned.

It was 'Hiya, Terry' everywhere I went, and I got a great welcome down at the Y.M.C.A. gym, renewing acquaintance with Lee Halfpenny. I don't suppose this fuss helped relationships with my trainer, who'd never been out of England with me and started resenting the Yanks. He couldn't see much good with America. As if this wasn't enough, while I was working-out at the Y.M.C.A. I was served with a writ from Cartier and Leavey, claiming they 'owned' my contract for four years. They succeeded in getting my purse-money for the Pender fight held in escrow—which meant I couldn't touch a cent. It was locked up.

Often sitting at my sister's home my back ached so badly I couldn't even watch TV sitting on a chair. I had to lie on the floor. I was in agony, physically and mentally, but I reckoned everything would work out O.K. when I moved into Boston for the full training. Although the back pain continued to nag enough to consider a postponement, I wasn't going to take the chance of blowing the fight for good.

As I trained harder it gradually grew less troublesome, though I was always scared it would come back at the wrong time. But on the night of the fight I can't claim I wasn't fit. I might have even been *too* fit!

When we went to Boston a character met us at the station who'd make the ideal part for a fight character in a film. He's Johnny Dunne, a cigar-chewing geezer, with dark features from Eye-tie stock and a leathery face. One look at him and I was entitled to be suspicious. He was sent by Sam Silverman, the promoter, to act as guide, bodyguard, assistant trainer, bag-carrier. I thought he was just a cab-driver. I figured this guy had to be rooting for Pender. But he was helpful and introduced me to every cop on the corner, the hotel bell-hops, and knew every layabout in the downtown gym. Ryder and I used to eye him up suspiciously and we even hid a couple of empty gin bottles so that we could take our own sealed water into the corner for the fight. We trusted nobody. It wouldn't have been hard for this Dunne geezer to nobble me with some stomach dope in the water.

Ryder ruled out the idea of Dunne helping out in the corner. Although I knew I'd never be upset by the American scene—I was one of the few British fighters who'd ever lived there before fighting for a world title—I reckoned to take out insurance and hire me a well-known American trainer just to be in my corner. I didn't really think it necessary, but you've got to think big in boxing if you want to survive. Harry Levene contacted Dan Florio, who flew in from New York. He had trained the oldest and youngest world heavy-weight champions, Jersey Joe Walcott and Floyd Patterson, and was a quiet, nice guy who knew the game. He didn't know me from Adam, but he'd do me. We gave him $300 for the night's work, plus expenses.

Looking back, I now know I'd been hard on Dunne, though he understood how I felt. But it didn't take me long to find out Johnny knew the fight business, had the ideas I liked, and we've struck up such a working friendship that I still fly Johnny from Boston to London to help me. So he's been well paid back. And he's a hellava good guy.

We stayed at the Somerset Hotel, on Commonwealth Avenue, and were treated well. But, blimey, it didn't 'arf look dodgy to me when I spotted the bell-captain—the head porter —was Pender's corner-man! But Leo Pratt, a nice little guy, had worked at the hotel long before I came on the scene. When he took me up in the elevator I used to kid him about getting ready to pick Pender up off the floor. But I couldn't afford to show any signs of edginess when Pratt was around. He was a good spy.

Yet despite being in Pender's home town, the people were terrific. I'll bet when fight-time came I had as many supporters as Pender. The people couldn't have been nicer, though I played along kidding about the notorious Boston fight decisions and having a ruckus with the Commission.

There was another upset. Two days before manager Sam Burns was due to leave with me from London he had a suspected heart-attack. This was the time I needed an experienced man to handle the local situation. There were a million engagements to arrange, people to meet or avoid, and I didn't want to be involved to spoil the training. So Sam sent a deputy— Harry Levene! I already had 'Trunky' Berry as a spar-mate and Harry brought Les Morgan, of Acton, with him. I think becoming a manager again gave Harry a great challenge. He revelled in it. Harry had worked as a young man on the circulation side of a New York paper and had handled Jock McAvoy and Dave Crowley in the States.

He knew the American scene well and had made many trips across the Atlantic. He was worldly, and wordy. I had Harry chasing around like a good 'un, fighting on my behalf. He frightened the life out of the Massachusetts Commission with all his arguments. The Board of Control had a Massachusetts Rule Book sent to them in advance of the fight so that we could discuss the differences. The Yanks altered rules by the hour.

I used to pull Levene's leg all the time, and it helped break the often tense atmosphere that gets into a fight camp. After each day's routine, with the fight approaching and nerves getting frayed, something was needed to break the strain. Harry was the fall-guy. He stood it well, because he'd been around long enough to know humouring a fighter is essential. I was grateful for Harry's help, which, I stress, was done for free.

I was regularly writing or phoning Sam Burns in London and saying I'd like him to fly over for the fight. I hated breaking up a happy team at the biggest moment of my life. Nobody is indispensable—it took me time to think of that word!—but I missed Sam. But even from his sick-bed Sam was scheming like a good 'un. He discovered Independent Television in London was going to show the fight-film and he contended that we'd signed only for the TV rights in America. Because of a friendship with Lew Grade, boss of the TV company concerned, the whole thing was settled without a fight. Grade sent Sam £1,000 compensation. Nothing could have been better timed to make Sam Burns feel better. He almost rolled out of bed and flew the Atlantic to Boston. I was right pleased to see him.

Although the purse-money—anything from £7,000 to £12,000—was being held, I was allowed reasonable expenses. Because I was using up the cash Pender's lawyer, Cronin, got the wind-up that if I won I'd forfeit the rest of the money and fight either Sugar Ray Robinson or Gene Fullmer, which would have been a bigger draw than meeting Pender again. He put the block on my spending spree. And that's where a real stand-up guy, George Parnassus, offered to come to the rescue.

Parnassus, the old silver-fox from Los Angeles, had flown in —and L.A. ain't just round the corner from Boston—offering to put up a $20,000 deposit for me. The weight of his influence was a help. There were no strings attached. Of course, he would have liked to have promoted a fight for me if I became champion, because he was running the biggest shows on the West Coast, with two world-title fights on one bill. It was Parnassus who paid Hogan Kid Bassey, of Nigeria, a fortune for three world-title fights in Los Angeles. I regret I never had the chance to fight for him.

Parnassus had emigrated as a kid from Greece to America to become a tailor. But he developed into a big-business operator with a steel company, besides being boxing's Mr. Big. His sons are a lawyer and a priest. Mr. P. is right proud of them. They had reason to be proud of him. No wonder they named a mountain in Greece after George Parnassus. He deserves it.

The sparring was going well down at the gym in Friend Street—that's a right name to have a sweat shop!—and I was smart taking my own sparring partners. Pender was offering £12 a day, and couldn't get them. Berry and Morgan made me work hard. I had to share the gym with Pender, who trained later, and all the wise guys would be there to weigh us up. I drew bigger crowds than Pender. My curiosity value was better. The dressing-room was no bigger than a telephone box, but the gym was well equipped with two rings, and it was handy for the local reporters to call in each day. I had to work hard one day to keep the fight on the front pages because the President-elect, John F. Kennedy, was in town, vote-collecting.

About a week before the fight I had my first bad word with a trainer. I'd never argued with anyone before. After four hard sparring rounds, with the partners coming up fresh for each round, Tom Ryder wanted to put me on the heavy bag. I refused. I was already a bit worn-out after the weeks of training and couldn't see the sense in belting into a heavy bag after sparring. 'All right, you know better than me,' he said, and we never discussed the disagreement again. It started an inevitable parting.

A fighter in my position had to have the right man. Training at home and training away were different kettles of fish. Tom was a good teacher, and I'd given him a gold watch as thanks after winning my Lonsdale Belt, but it was no use to me if he carried a chip on his shoulder. He just wouldn't fit into the routine in America. He resented everything about the set-up.

But in no way could I complain about my fighting condition, except for the twinge still creeping into my back. At the time I'd trained harder than before, though road-work was not easy with ice and heavy snow clogging up the roads. Looking back, I feel I might have over-trained—and that was the opinion of Dan Florio from the moment he saw me shape-up in the fight.

Pender and I met at a reception given by the promoter in the swank Darbury Rooms, then we both had a medical check-up at the Commission offices, which they called the Public Department of Safety! I geared-up like a Cockney lumberjack, while Pender looked more like a City gent in grey suit and gold watch. Peter Wilson, always on the scene, sent a report home which said: 'Of all the British champions whom I have travelled to watch on the American continent Terry Downes is easily the most confident.' He sounded more confident than me.

A Dr. Francis J. Wixted, of the Commission, gave us the usual thorough check and I kidded when he ordered the eye test by reading a calendar on the wall instead of the sight test card. Then the managers and the Press went into conference with the chairman, Herman Greenberg, a local trade-union boss, Tommy Rawson, a public works contractor, and Eddie Urbec, a drug-store salesman whom I'd last seen refereeing at the Olympics in Rome.

Harry Levene had his say and we were told that Pender's rabbit-punching would be watched, that we'd wear 8 oz. gloves, and that two judges and a referee of the highest integrity (what's that?) would be appointed. Like it made any difference to me. When you're playing away from home you have to take what's coming. I daresay half the wool they were pulling over my eyes was cotton, but they meant well. (Just to show how completely unbiased the Commission were, two of them went to England later as guests of Pender and Cronin, and one of them was shouting like a good 'un for Pender against me at Wembley from a second-row press seat—and I've got a dozen witnesses to prove it! Whatever I moan about Britain's Board,

I'll bet nobody has ever heard an official yelling for their own fighter. They don't stick up enough for us!)

But if I didn't win well I didn't want no favours. I didn't figure to outpoint Pender, anyway, because point-nicking with boxing was his game, so mine had to be fighting. Mind you, his left hand was enough to cover my face, because the gloves we wore weighed *10* oz. each, two more than oridnary amateur gloves in Britain and four more than pro. They felt like pillow-cases. I've got my pair at home and would have a tough job knocking the old woman over with 'em.

A plane-load of supporters from London poured in, including Harry Grossmith and Ivor Barnard, who had promoted some of my small-hall fights in London. Cousin Pat also brought the flash dressing-gown I'd forgotten to pack. All told, I had Barbara, Sylvie, my brother-in-law in from Baltimore with Dad, and four cousins from London. We were mob-handed, but still under the cosh compared with Pender's Boston Irish.

Another surprise visitor was Terry Spinks, the feather-weight champion, who volunteered to give me a work-out for speed. The Board of Control sent secretary Teddy Waltham, who was trying to iron out any rule differences and would sit in Pender's dressing-room when they bandaged his hands. It was all very comforting, but I'm a realist. Nothing mattered unless I could fight well.

At the weigh-in I knew Waltham was wasting his time when he questioned the scales—both of us weighed in at exactly the limit—and some guy yelled out, 'You ain't in England now.' The friendship stuff was over. The Americans, whether they liked Pender or not, weren't keen on losing their title.

Just as I had conquered the nerve situation—I didn't care two cents for nobody—they succeeded in stacking the odds against me at the weigh-in. Writs from Leavey and Cartier were dished out like tea biscuits. Apart from me, writs were bunged to Silverman, Pender, the three Massachusetts commissioners, my mum and dad, Sam Burns, Harry Levene, Teddy Waltham, and the Gillette Razor Co. (the TV sponsors).

Pender was thirty, six years older than me, and had been fighting twelve years. He'd retired about four times, complaining that his hands were too brittle. They called him putty fists. But none of the guys who got into a ring with Pender, including Sugar Ray, Gene Fullmer, Carmen Basilio, and me, reckoned him a soft puncher. S'all right for those outside the ropes to judge—I'm telling you from inside. He was a stand-up boxer, with long arms, a typical British style (his ancestors came from Killarney), and had forty-four fights.

We were different as chalk from cheese except that we'd both served in the Marines. It made me feel right proud when they paraded us into the ring at Boston Arena, a shabby joint compared with Wembley, with Marine escorts, and they presented arms inside the ring when the British and U.S. anthems were played. Me and Pender stood to attention and stared at each other. This was tension time. I'd goaded him a bit, hoping he'd try slugging it out with me. But I'd never underestimated him. Anyone who stays thirty rounds with Sugar Ray ain't no mug.

They made such a play about Pender's supposedly bad hands that I was fully prepared for a right good whack at the start. And I got it! While I was looking at Pender's left hand, the punch he used best, he cracked me on the chin with a handsome right-hander. As I fell back, Pender fell over me with the force he'd put into the punch. Apart from the whack, the fact that Pender fell on me made sure I'd go down. I'd tried grabbing his arms, but my legs shot up in the air and for a couple of seconds I didn't know where the hell I was.

I could see a lot of lights, a few stars, and hear a thousand voices yelling. Then I realized what had happened and thought to myself, 'You idiot, fancy standing for a punch like that.' I was so embarrassed being on the floor in the first round after all the boasting I'd done. I felt a right wash-out. The knock-down made me madder than I should have been. I got up at seven and steamed into him.

I knew I'd already got a lot to make up and perhaps I did things I wouldn't have done if I hadn't been on the deck. I don't kid myself I'm a Fancy Dan at the best of times, but I was walking in more reckless than ever. I was pig-headed and wanted to do it my way. The crowd were going mad and a lot of them were on my side. He never got much of a chance to plant another right-hander on the chin for the rest of the round because I was too busy chasing him. I went back to the corner as right as ninepence.

Pender liked to throw his arms around me and grab a breather whenever he could. All his good stuff was done in spasms. I'd managed to get the film of Pender's fight with Robinson—it's handy to have the right connections!—and I'd gone into the fight heartened because I noticed even with a slower Robinson that Pender was always looking for a rest. I figured I'd bustle him until he really ran out of gas.

I was surprised how easy I could hit Pender, because I'd figured him to be a smarter boxer. Whenever I crowded, where I could do a bit of damage, he grabbed real good, and the referee, Bill Connelly (a local cop who didn't like scuffles!), yanked me off. Once I clouted Pender on the break, which at that time was legal in England, and since they kept telling me Boston was 'English' I reckoned it O.K. With me it's no holds barred.

If I could stop Pender holding I'd be half-way home and if he thought he'd get a nice whack coming out of a clinch maybe he wouldn't be so keen. But the referee clutched me around the throat. 'Aye, aye,' I thought, 'I've got one here.' I knew then I wasn't gonna get any favours. I never saw the referee touch Pender, but I got plenty of shoves.

I got over the first-round knock-down and because I was piling on the punches I felt Pender grunting and groaning when I got in close. He was fighting like a man who didn't fancy the job. Maybe he'd sold me short and I'm sure he wasn't as fit as me. His mouth came open a lot. I got a little cut around the eye in the second, but in the third he gashed my nose right across the bridge. It looked just as though he'd cracked my hooter with an axe. The blood spurted out like a fountain. 'Blimey,' I thought, 'we're off again! I'll have to do something now to catch up with this geezer.'

When I got back to the corner they had to scarper around stuffing their fingers in my mouth, on my nose, over the eye, sponging me down, sweating and talking, while I'm trying to suck some fresh air. This is the seconds' hard-graft time. But they're smart. If you don't believe me just watch how quick they dive *out* of the ring when the bell goes! But with all that messing about I was glad to hear the bell go and get out for some peace. It's quieter in the clinches.

Florio, who tried first, and then Ryder, who insisted on having a go, could not stop the nose-blood flow. I looked like a Red Indian. But I thought it was a bit much after the second round when the Commission doctor came into the corner to examine my cut eye, which wasn't even a handicap. I called that hustling. That encouraged the referee to start coming to the corner between rounds, which didn't exactly boost my confidence. The doctor and referee had two conferences. They had a right chat at my expense. After the sixth, when my corner-men knew I couldn't go on, they sent me out to throw everything. The doctor had marked my card by saying loudly to the referee, 'If the blood keeps flowing, call it off.' It had to be my last-round fling.

Yet I still didn't think Pender, on the night, was really better than me. He boxed pretty good, but definitely his legs were buckling whenever I belted him around the body. In the fourth, a round I won, I knocked Pender's gumshield flying. I was hoping his teeth had come out with it. Blimey, I didn't 'arf need a bit of encouragment.

Pender might have been tired, but I was the one who looked like I'd been through a meat-grinder, though a bit of blood wasn't stopping me from throwing everything I'd got. Trouble was, I knew if I couldn't catch up with Pender quick it was big odds the cut would get worse. And it did. The blood pumped out of the ole hooter like an artery had been cut. After fifty-seven seconds of the seventh round the referee stepped in. I couldn't go on. My hooter had let me down. Pender won by a nose.

I came out with a lot of glory, looking gory, and the usual hospital case. Dr. Kelsey, who went mainly to support me, stripped off and got cracking in the hotel room. I ended up getting twelve stitches on my nose in the local hospital, with one for luck on my eyebrow.

Pender was puffing and blowing in his dressing-room and

telling reporters I was the gamest guy he'd fought. Pender
was a good pro. I had nothing against him. We wound up
getting plenty of money together.

There were arguments all over Boston that I'd have won
but for being cut. My supporters couldn't see it any other way.
But just in case you think it's all bias, I can tell you my dad
was chatting in the hotel lobby with fans and reporters and
telling them he thought I wasn't myself and Pender would
probably have won! He reckoned Pender a great boxer who
had my measure.

We Downeses don't kid to nobody. I knew I was slow getting
off with a punch and that first-round wallop didn't do me any
good, but I still thought I could have won. From my corner
seat I gave Pender three rounds, me two, and one even.

Harry Markson, a level-headed man who is boss of boxing
at Madison Square Garden, said he thought body-punching
was a lost art and he never expected to see an Englishman
showing the American that he is master at it. Markson offered
me a fight in the Garden and name my own opponent. Even
wonderful press quotes by Jack Dempsey and Rocky Marciano,
who both reckoned I was winning, didn't cheer me up. I was
sad inside. Losing is a great blow to me. Being cut seemed
crueller.

The English writers came around to see me, as usual, and I
tossed a dollar on the floor and said that was all I'd got for my
troubles. The purse-money, which would be more than £6,000,
was frozen-up pending my law case. The promotion hadn't
broken any records because Pender hadn't done much shouting
and all my hooting beforehand was a lost cause. They didn't
even have programmes printed. Sam Silverman promoted out
of a suitcase. Although he had offices alongside a Boston market-
place, he and his missus used to lug a suitcase-load of tickets
around with them and sell 'em like street-corner dealers. I
always had the feeling Sam had the case packed ready to blow
town at a minute's notice.

But Silverman was what the Yanks call a regular guy. I
liked him. Naturally he'd be rooting a bit for Pender, but I
got every concession I asked for. Sam had been around the

business for many years and gave the impression that nobody knew the trouble he'd seen. He's a fat, red-faced geezer, who holds his drink good, chain smokes cigars, and if he spots a shack in any part of New England he'll try running a show.

Rocky Marciano owed a lot to Silverman. He promoted thirty-one of his forty-nine fights. And Sam must be a game guy. A few years ago because he was operating independently the powerful promoting combines weren't too pleased about it. So somebody dropped a bomb in the basement of Sam's home. Nice people. Luckily, Sam was out at the time. A few days later his wife was lucky enough to be called to the phone when a bullet whizzed through a kitchen window.

As if this wasn't enough, poor old Sam, who ain't exactly a Hercules, got nicely beaten-up in the street. So you see life ain't all hay for a promoter in the States. He survived everything and today is still top man in New England. Boxing would be dead there without him.

At home the news was broken with the *Daily Mirror* covering the front page with a photo of Barbara kissing me and Peter Wilson's two-page story headed: 'Blood and Guts! Spirit is Willing, but Flesh is Weak.' Yet there was just one consolation in all the thousands of words describing the fight. Al Lacey, who had trained Pender, told the British reporters that I was sure to become a world champion. Lacey, in his sixties, had worked with Jack Sharkey right on to Pender and Carlos Ortiz. I have the highest regard for him. And it was Lacey's decision that afterwards made me the champion of the world! It was also chiefly because of his experience as a corner-man, I am sure, that pumped-up Pender to regain his title.

So Al was no pal.

Champion of the World

I LEFT America reckoning I'd had it for another crack at the world title. The Yanks ain't keen on giving too many chances to foreigners, not because they're scared but because they liked to keep title fights circulating in the States. Let's face it, they've had the best fighters for years, so you can't blame them for being cocky.

I had a consolation when Harry Levene said in America he'd offer $100,000, about £35,000, for Pender to fight me at Wembley. To encourage Pender to come away from home he also agreed to 'cut in' Silverman on a London show. I was the only geezer who thought Levene was serious. Most of the papers laughed it off. The *Daily Herald* called it 'A Lot of Hot Air'. Old Harry had the last laugh. He signed the return for Wembley six months later. But it cost him about a £5,000 loss to get me the title.

Believe me, settling all the business took best part of six months—and there were still arguments going on until an half-hour before we went into the ring!

Silverman and Pender's mouthpiece, John Cronin, flew from Boston to start negotiations, and, with Levene, Astaire, and Burns, were locked up in a suite at the Grosvenor House for virtually three days and nights before they even got to near agreement. The champion nearly always calls the deal and Pender was guaranteed $84,000 (that's about three quid short of £30,000) plus $20,000 (£7,142) for Silverman as his share.

Because the British Board of Control bar the return-clause contracts for fights in this country, Cronin had a better idea. He demanded—and got—another $35,000 (£12,499) deposited in an American bank in London as a security for a third fight in the event of me becoming champion.

This is what they call a hold-up job, nice and legal, take it or leave it. You either pay up or forget the fight. None of the jolly-good-sport stuff matters, or Englishman's-word-is-his-bond crap. Astaire stuck the money up and I indemnified him as a safeguard. My end of the purse would come from the gate-takings. The fight, of course, would not be televised live. We did pretty good with the price for the film rights.

Despite all the ends being sewn up, I was not prepared to hang around without a fight for six months. Even if I did keep putting my nose in the way, I thrived on fighting. Harry Levene had the right idea keeping me in front of the public and the first opponent was Wild Willie Green, a part Indian from Rhode Island, who had sparred regularly with Pender.

Green, at twenty-three, was a has-been. Truth is he looked a never-waser. But he'd won twenty-three of twenty-six fights. Strong as a bull, but not too clever at the boxing lark, he suited me down to the ground. My nose had healed up well and I'd given it a run-out in the gym. The fight was at Wembley and I'd got into terrific shape. I took a look at Green for a round and a half, just flicking out punches and playing it smart. He grabbed a bit and a couple of his punches stung, so I figured I'd open up and get him out of the way a bit lively.

If I couldn't do a good job on Green I reckoned I had no right worrying about Pender again. I wouldn't be worth the return fight. So I performed at a fair ole pace, bouncing the Yank all round the ring. But he ducked and shoved his head into me to get a warning and I figured this geezer was gonna make me look bad. After the second round I shoved him aside to get back to the corner. While the seconds were telling me to get on with the job I was weighing Green up.

In the third a cracking left hook had him wobbling and I started pitching him from pillar to post when the referee stepped in. It was a nice, well-paid work-out. No blood or bruises. One more like that and I'd be right for Pender.

So Levene, who wasn't looking to get me knocked off, offered another good pay-day to meet Tony Montano from

Arizona, a part Mexican-Indian fighter managed by Bill Swift, the meat millionaire who handled Zora Folley. Montano had had about thirty fights and had been knocking around the training camps of Don Jordan and Ray Robinson without causing any bother. He'd do me fine.

To be fair, Levene wouldn't stand for the fight being top of the bill, but sharing with Terry Spinks v. Howard Winstone for the feather-weight title. Since Harry had forked out £12,055 to buy that fight, I was entitled to keep quiet.

I thought Harry had gone a bit potty paying that kinda money, with me and Montano not exactly getting peanuts. Shows how wrong you can be. The place was packed. My mate Spinks blew his title, because he was too weak at the weight, and Winstone speeded Spinks out of it to poke his head off.

My fight ain't worth remembering, except that Montano was cut-up instead of me and I boxed well within myself making the Yank retire after five rounds.

July 11, 1961, was the date set for Pender v. Downes at Empire Pool, Wembley, and I set up my training camp at the Parachute Regiment Territorial Army gym at White City. Americans Eddie Machen and Joe Brown were the only other fighters to have used the drill hall. After me Cassius Clay trained there. It was ideal.

Although Tom Ryder had been getting about 10 per cent of my purse-money as trainer when I won and 7½ per cent when I lost, things weren't what they used to be between him and me. I told him I reckoned £400 for the fight was a fair pay-day. After all, he didn't have to leave home to train me. He came and rubbed me down after morning running at Hampstead Heath and spent the odd hour in the gym in the afternoon.

Naturally, I figured Tom's pride wouldn't accept these kind of money deals in future and after the Pender fight we parted. It was better than having a row. We both left each other without any hard feelings.

I met Pender again at a lunch Levene organized at the Dorchester Hotel, which is Harry's 'local'. He lives next door. I tried to do a bit of goading to liven the show, but it was no use doing all the shouting if Pender wouldn't shout back. He was nicely satisfied copping his guarantee and couldn't care less.

That's the one thing that made Pender a poor champion in my book. He was strictly him first. Because he kept quiet, Levene had trouble flogging his tickets in midsummer when other sports were going big and claiming most of the publicity.

But, with me, winning the title mattered more than all else. I recruited a right hard bunch of sparring-partners at the army gym—including Randolph Turpin! But bringing Randy in for a day was just a stunt and a bit of boost for me. I was the first Britisher to fight for the world middle-weight championship at home since Turpin toppled Sugar Ray Robinson at Earls Court in 1951. Ten years later Randy was running a little café at Leamington, messing around the wrestling game, and never seen around the fight halls. He came to London on a day-excursion ticket.

He'd written some articles saying he was practically broke and how little he got out of his fight earnings. When you reckon up that Turpin and Robinson, for their second fight in New York, drew the record gate receipts for a non-heavy-weight match—$992,630—and Randy's reported gross share was $207,075—about £84,000!—it seemed not only ridiculous but shameful that he had to resort to stunt-boxer v. wrestler matches and earning a few bob getting in the ring with Terry Downes.

Mug's game or not, you can bet your bottom dollar I'll not be asking for any charity at any time in my life. My loot, a lot of it hard-earned, is tied up lock, stock, and barrel. I'll never be short.

Because Turpin wasn't licensed to fight, the Board of Control clamped down in their own high-hat way and refused to let Turpin officially spar with me. They don't allow non-licensed fighters to become sparring-partners because it can't be too clever for their health. That's fair enough, but Turpin didn't need any protection. Just a round at half-speed for the photographers proved Randy a smashing whacker. He tucked me a punch up the ribs to make me realize what a good champ he must have been.

When we were messing about in that empty White City

hall I wondered just how much money we could have pulled if we'd been fighting at the same time. Could I have beaten Turpin? How can anyone really say? All I know is it would have been one hellava fight!

The others who were regular in the camp were Wally Swift, of Nottingham, who was welter-weight champion, George Aldridge, who became middle-weight champion, Bob Nicolson, of Farnborough, who trained on to become area champion, Gerry McNally, and dear old Johnny Berry, champion of nowhere but a right hard customer.

I needed Swift to box every day to get practice dodging left-hands. He could use a left a bit like Pender. Everything went fine and the training was timed almost to the second, from the early-morning runs to the rub-down after the sparring. I don't think anyone could have worked harder, and Barbara had the job of turning out any visitors at home when the clock reached 9.30.

I went to bed like clockwork, so for months on end our home life got right regimented. It was difficult to explain to strangers, and even friends, that to be successful you have to stick hard at it and no liberties. A half-fit fighter can get himself a nice whacking. Without fitness I was a dead duck.

But, just my luck, on the very last day of sparring, about four days before the fight, I cracked heads in a clinch with Wally Swift and tore the skin off my nose! I flung off my headguard as though somebody had kicked me in the guts. This was too ridiculous to be true. Luckily there were no reporters about and the sparring-partners said nothing. But I was sick to the heart. I mean, how much was I supposed to take?

We managed to put a patch over the hooter—a sort of silencer!—and right away they've sniffed out the news in Fleet Street. I detest having to lie to anyone, especially the newspaper fellahs, because it's hard to look them in the face when they know you're fannying. But I had to face this one out. I told them I'd been given a special prescription to keep on my nose a few days because it hardened the skin.

It was some special jollop made up in Harley Street at a pound an ounce, I told them. But dear old Ernie Jarvis was

L

pressing me a bit and even insisted on having a photographer at my home to take the pictures of Barbara putting the 'special gear' on the nose.

I felt a right Charley trying to act this one out, but I still never took off the covering and made Barbara pose like an actress without a blush. Oh, if only Ernie had known the truth! There was even a scab on the nose two days before the fight. Joe Bloom, who owned the Cambridge Gymnasium in the West End before Sam Burns leased it from him, was a bit of a crackpot with potions and he'd been giving me some hardening-up mixture to plaster on my nose.

Mind you, I felt a right berk when I found out Joe had stuck a cracked lavatory-pan with the same gear!

Luckily, come fight time, we managed to clean up the skin and powder the ole nose like a pansy. But I'd laid on a doctor and a fast car—just in case. The weigh-in was organized in style at a theatre restaurant—that day me and Pender were Talk of the Town!—and he looked well, turning up with bowler and rolled umbrella. One thing I like about the Yanks, they can't believe every Englishman don't carry an umbrella or was educated at Eton. They soon found out different when I unloaded my accent on 'em.

While I'd had my hooter troubles, I'd heard Pender wasn't having everything his own way, either. His wife was expecting, which always worries a fighter when away from home, and he'd had a stomach upset by the change in food and water. But he looked fit enough at the weigh-in, with me just a ¼ lb. lighter than him at 11 st. 4¾ lb. We both made the championship weight easily. But there was bother with Pender and the stipulated amount of hand bandages allowed for a title fight. A fighter with banged-up hands needs every inch he can get, even though it don't help all that much. I think it just feels safer with hands well padded up.

Let me say I couldn't have cared less how much bandage Pender used, so long as he didn't shove a horseshoe in the gloves, but I got mad because I knew letters had been sent to our Board from Pender's camp demanding extra use of bandage —or he wouldn't fight!

I'd been shoved around from coal-hole to breakfast-time in Boston, fighting to their rules, but Pender could still call the tune in England. It was the principle that annoyed me. Whose side were the Board of Control on? Less than an hour before the fight there were ructions going on in the Wembley dressing-rooms. Anyone who thought the bandages argument was just a publicity stunt soon changed their mind when they knew about the arguments after the show had started.

In Britain a Board inspector watches the bandaging procedure ordered by the Board for all championship or eliminating fights. Then he stamps each hand so that no extra can be smuggled on before the gloves are tied in the ring. I've always reckoned this practice a right laugh.

You can go around little halls of the country and I've seen any amount of bandages and plaster shoved on hands with nobody caring. Suddenly everyone becomes a big-shot with a championship fight. It's the little guys who need protection—not champions.

Anyway, I'm already bandaged up, but Pender refused the length and the quality of the Board's 'issue' bandages. Onslow Fane, the Board president, and Teddy Waltham, the secretary, were scurrying about the dressing-rooms trying to settle the argument. As far as I was concerned there was no argument. Pender agreed to fight in this country, probably for more money than he was worth, under our rules. But he told officials, point-blank, that unless he was allowed to use his own bandages he would walk out. I think he would, too. I remember Waltham coming to ask me what I thought. 'You're supposed to be the Board of Control,' I said. 'You tell him what to do. What is it here? I boxed under Boston rules, now you lay the law down.'

I can just imagine what would have happened to me if I'd caused the Board that trouble. I'd have been sweeping-up Oxford Street and suspended for life. Refusing to fight half an hour before a fight is ridiculous. The worse way, I reckoned, Pender was entitled to be suspended after the fight, especially as the Board are supposed to have an agreement with the New York Commission.

But we British are great boys for giving up quietly. Pender

won the argument and wore his own bandages. The Board had amended a thirty-two-year-old rule for him.

I tell you I was sick with this argument and being a loser before I started in my own country. And, to rub it in, Ike Powell, the referee who had disqualified me against McCormack, was appointed.

I went into the ring with a bit of needle, and remembering how Pender was puffing in the Boston fight, even though he had things going for him, I fancied I could pressure him better this time. Pender was 7—4 favourite because he had not lost for nine years!

Because of the difference in style, me and Pender would always have made a good fight. Yet, surprisingly, this one didn't turn out all that exciting. The occasion helped create the atmosphere but I'd had better punch-ups on the way to the title.

I was determined to take things steadier, but was dead worried the nose would let me down. I felt Pender out for the first round, but he caught me a few fair left jabs in the second and suddenly I felt the blood trickling down the nose.

I can't explain the sinking feeling I got, but when I got back to the corner Tom Ryder, Sam Burns, and a new helper, Danny Vary, nerveless and as cold as ice, all said it was just a scratch. They patched it up well.

Then I fancied showing off and switched styles to boxing and, honest, I caught Pender with plenty of straight lefts. He was a sucker for them. I nailed him with a good left hook and the crowd didn't arf roar when Pender went sagging back, but before I could pile on some more punches he grabbed and fiddled me out of it.

Pender was a clever geezer and again fought only in spasms. He had a nice style, though, which appealed more to English fans than Americans. I varied my work from a bit of fancy boxing to a bit of rough fighting. Pender honestly looked upset and I was certain about the fourth round that I'd got his number.

Naturally, I couldn't duck everything and I had a small nick under the left eye and it began to swell. But Pender's right eye was cut. Although we kept things going pretty evenly, he always wobbled more than me under pressure. He caught me some good whacks, but they never bothered me. I felt Pender was thieving points rather than fighting like a champion.

In the sixth round Pender tried the old dodge of darting up from his stool and coming at me. I thought to myself, 'Come on, mate, that's my game,' and steamed straight into him. If I could really open Pender up he was a gonna for sure. I dropped him, as much from a shove as a punch, in the sixth and he got up without any bother at 'two'. It was the only time either of us looked like going down.

Whenever I pressed Pender back on the ropes he felt as weak as a kitten, but he could counter-punch good and the crowd loved his get-out-of-trouble counters. But the more I could get him to fight, the less chance I knew he had.

Pender, though he might not have looked it, was a pretty fair banger. Between the Boston and Wembley fights he had fought Carmen Basilio, a right hard egg, and finished his career by dropping him. But my fitness and style, with age on my side, bothered Pender. When his eyebrow leaked more blood I started ducking under his guard and belting away like a good 'un. He was definitely getting desperate. My left eye was closing, but I could see him well enough to know he was in worse shape than me.

In the ninth he came out throwing everything and I kept the guard up, saying to myself, 'That's it, mate, you keep going and punch yourself out because I can go on for ever at this lark.' Pender fought terrific in that round—because it was his last! People made me laugh asking why he looked so good yet retired on his stool at the end of the round. If I'd known it was gonna be my last round I promise you I'd have looked better than him.

As the ninth bell ended I laughed in his face, as much as to say, 'If that's the best you can do just wait until I get going,' but I never got the chance. He flopped on his stool, fagged out, and Al Lacey called the referee over to the corner. 'He can't go on,' said Lacey. 'His eye is bad and the boy is through.'

The crowd couldn't believe it when Powell accepted the

retirement and came over to my corner and raised my hand. I was, naturally, a bit surprised, yet I'd half suspected him quitting. I said in Boston he didn't fight as though he really liked the job, though he had me cut up.

Mobs came around the ringside and I had a tougher time getting back to the dressing-room than fighting Pender. Surrendering on the stool left a bad taste and in many ways robbed me of a real bit of glory. Don't make the slightest mistake about it, at Wembley that night I'd have stopped Pender in style if he'd gone on. He quit because I'd made him quit.

I'm not denying that maybe he wasn't 100 per cent fit because Lacey told a story later about having to give Pender injections for a cold a few days before the fight. Maybe it was an off night. But only maybe. I broke his heart because he couldn't hurt me.

I also heard a lot of rubbish talked that maybe he packed up easy because he knew we had a return fight signed. Or even that gamblers had made a killing. What a load of rubbish! No champion will 'loan' a title, it's too risky. I could have got out of the return fight any time I wanted and it would still have been profitable foregoing the deposit. I was offered a fortune to meet Gene Fullmer or Ray Robinson in the States. Californian promoter, Walter Minskoff, sent his match-maker to London with a $100,000 banker's draft for me to fight Sugar.

Gambling? Don't make me laugh. If you get more than a few quid on a fight everyone knows about it. The betting-boys are not mugs. Sam Silverman and a buddy from Boston who bets big came over with a nice few thousand dollars to put on *Pender*. I know some of the people who took some of their money. Know what happened? Sam was unable to get all the money 'on' and made it known afterwards that he was pleased with the get-out, which meant in gambling terms he'd actually saved money.

And another reason why it didn't suit Silverman for Pender to lose with a bit of disgrace was because it ruined Pender's name in the States.

Poor ole Sam got a belting in more ways than one. I went down to the Pigalle, in the West End, with a big family mob for a celebration. But I was so full of the world I couldn't sit still, so Barbara and me left after about half-hour to drive around until the early hours. When I got home a keen photographer was waiting on my doorstep.

Meanwhile, Silverman was apparently at a restaurant nearby and was called outside by a couple of disgruntled gamblers, who planted a right-hander on Sam's jaw and gave him a kicking to go with it. Nice people. But ole Sam dusted himself down like nothing had happened and when the police asked him to press charges for assault he said he couldn't identify the attackers. And if ever Sam says he got a kick out of his visit to London you'll know he ain't kidding!

Whenever a fight turns out a shock result we always get the stupid chat about a fix. It takes too much to fix a fight and in all my travels and chat with fellow fighters I've never heard of one fixed fight. I know of plenty of bad matches, and times when a fighter has 'swallowed it'—which means he's gone down too easily—but only because he knows he'll get a bigger hiding staying up.

But, generally, fighters have got terrific pride. Winning always means too much and, like I say, the moment any real money is bet on a fight in Britain the whole world knows about it. Mind you, don't ask me to fathom out the Sonny Liston and Cassius Clay result in Miami Beach, because that was a fight too stupid for even me to comment. Before the fight you had to pick Liston, especially after Henry Cooper had stuck Clay on the deck at Wembley. And the way Liston quit in the corner still makes me suspicious. But who am I to doubt half a dozen doctors who said Sonny's arm was injured?

The Press went to town with my capture of the world championship, even though I thought they overdid the tributes to gameness and not enough credit for ability. I had the chance to say so. Members of the Boxing Writers' Club threw a luncheon in my honour at the Café Royal and presented me with a photo of Britain's only three world middle-weight champions—Bob Fitzsimmons, Randolph Turpin, and me. It was inscribed 'Britain's Big Three'. It was a proud moment and though I didn't always agree with the critics I couldn't complain with the way I was treated. I was really honoured being rated 'Sportsman of the Year' by the Sportswriters' Association.

Somebody had said I should have retired a long time ago, a lot of people were saying I wouldn't last six months after they watched my first few fights, but there I was addressing the critics as world champion. It's a great feeling. I still felt the Press were underplaying me as though they begrudged the win. I've often felt this way reading of other sports victories. Maybe it's the British way of life. Everyone ain't as brash as me. But, for God sake, don't be ashamed when we come up with a winner. Let's rub the losers' noses into the ground. All that jolly-good-loser jazz makes me laugh. I'd made Pender hold and run for his life, and forced him to quit. What else could I do to deserve credit? More had been written about him quitting than me winning!

But the thing that really got my goat was the commentary of the TV film given by Fred Verlander. I reckoned it nothing short of diabolical. I've got the film and have watched it maybe forty times and I'll still never get accustomed to hearing Verlander say, 'It's all Pender,' even when I'm belting him right on the nose. I showed the film in the States to reporters, and even rabid Pender fans, when I went back for the third fight.

Without exception they all thought the commentary was completely misleading. One American said, 'I've heard of the British being sporting, but this is ridiculous.' To listen you'd think I wasn't even in the fight. But at no time could there have been more than fractions between us.

I wish commentators would realize their responsibility. One distorted report, even when people can see, can mislead. No doubt Verlander knows boxing, because he was the army team-coach. But knowing it and speaking it is a big difference. With me, he's an amateur.

I like Harry Carpenter's chat with TV fights, especially about how many kids a fighter has or when he last shaved. Like it all makes a difference? Harry's a bit touchy about a bit of blood and makes a play of it. Still I've got the option of turning the sound off.

I like listening to David Coleman's TV talk; he's a right lad and whenever he's interviewed me we've never bothered with scripts. It's strictly playing it by ear. Peter Dimmock, the B.B.C. Sportsview boss, is a bit pompous and looks like he should do a double act with a tailor's dummy.

When I've been around Dimmock's studio it looks like they got too many chiefs and not enough Indians. I get the impression Dimmock does us fighters a favour talking to us. Makes no difference. I can't understand him and I doubt if he can understand me. He chats like he's got a plum in his mouth and I chat like I'm chewing it!

The greatest with me is Eamonn Andrews. I'll back him against anyone in the world for fight broadcasting. He don't romance to make it sound like a good fight. Maybe that's because Eamonn was a fair old amateur fighter himself.

A big bonus came my way after becoming champion. I had been granted a licence to change our car showroom, in Manor Road, Harlesden, to a betting shop. I was on my way to becoming a tycoon—but didn't know it. The betting laws had been lifted a few months before, so that bets could be legally placed at licensed premises. Only the town-planning licence was stopping me and cousin Pat from opening the shop. We soon got it.

Neither of us knew a thing about betting odds. But I was too restless to worry about employing an experienced settler, though Sam Burns, who was then working as an executive with the Willim Hill (the world's biggest) betting organization, advised us against going it alone. But I couldn't fling the doors open quick enough and it was a right carry-on with bets being made out and me counting the money. I thought this was a game and a half.

Jarvis Astaire telephoned a £5 win-treble bet 'just for luck', so we'd made a big start. But at the end of the day his bet had won and we'd been skinned alive by the winning favourites to lose £70! Pat and I wished we were back in the car game. I thought all bookies were supposed to be winners.

I'd got into the betting-shop business before manager Burns, and later, with an idea of giving my dad an interest, I opened

a licensed gambling club, converting a billiard-hall, in Harlesden. It's still going strong, though it's now a bigger social night
out than spieling.

What I did to sprout out in business I did on my own, stand
or fall, but I couldn't reckon when I began that Burns and me
would grow into an 'empire' and benefit by a big take-over. . . .
We made £40,000 in our first full year and over £80,000 in
our second year. With Jarvis Astaire, well versed in the world
of high finance, advising me and acting for us, Hurst Park
Syndicate, the company that had owned the famous racecourse,
then paid Sam Burns and me £180,000, with the same amount
in ordinary shares. We had to agree to serve as executives, Sam
becoming a director of the company and me bound for three
years.

We own, under the deal, 750,000 deferred shares which can
be changed into ordinary shares when profits climb to £127,000
before tax and the dividend to 13½ per cent. It was a nice few
bob without even taking a punch!

Caning Sugar Ray

CHAMPION of the world, I'm on top of the world, and we're already considering the date for the showdown battle in Boston. At no time did I ever consider running out of the agreement, though Pender and Silverman got dead worried. We reckoned the third match would be in September, just two months later. So I took a quick rest in Spain and got down to road-work the day I returned.

On daughter Wendy's birthday I must have been all fatherly excited by getting up first to creep down to the hall and collect her birthday cards. I tripped on the stairs (I usually like the day to wear itself out before I take it on!) and jarred my thumb. It made me feel sick and a bit dizzy. Within an hour my thumb started swelling and after a conference with Sam Burns we decided to get specialist attention from Bill Tucker, an orthopaedic expert who treats many sportsmen—and the Queen Mother.

I'd thrown a thousand punches and never seriously hurt a hand. But that trip caused me more pain than any hurts in the ring. After an injection the thumb reddened and swelled up like a cricket ball. It was a shocking pain. On a Sunday morning Tucker sent me to London Homoeopathic Hospital— and I was back on the operating table! Mr. Donald Brooks was the specialist.

They carved a nice slice out of the thumb, which had become poisoned, and scraped down to the bone. A specialist told me that if I had left the operation another twenty-four hours I could easily have lost my thumb. Charming thought.

In America they were accusing me of ducking out of the

fight with a faked injury. It seemed to them like a stroke. Nobody in boxing believes the truth, but scandal spreads fast. It wasn't until I got a visit from General Krulewitch, chairman of the New York State Commission, that Pender was convinced. Me and the old General got on fine. He was an old Leatherneck—with a better job than me—and I was really pleased when he presented me with a pair of Marine cufflinks.

I was stuck in hospital, arm raised like a strap-hanger on a train to have the fluid drained off. Pender was lucky I recovered to fight him within six months of the Wembley surrender—because I had more trouble in store.

For two solid months I attended a clinic every day for electrical vibration and remedial treatment. At first I'd lost complete use of the thumb. I thought I was finished.

Because Pender was pestering the Board of Control I was called to explain the delay.

We passed some correspondence around the table and I wanted to pass my thumb around to show the scar. Again I got the feeling the Board were on Pender's side more than mine. I didn't want to be lazing around while a fortune waited for me in America. When we eventually settled a date, the Board, despite taking a fair whack of my best purses over the years, wouldn't send a representative to act on my behalf in Boston. It was disgusting. So, like a mug, I agreed to pay £100 towards the air fare of Board secretary Teddy Waltham. He reminded me in a broadcast later that he'd helped to protect my interests in Boston, but forgot to mention I was part paying for the service. And don't let's kid ourselves. The Yanks listened—but still did exactly what they wanted! Waltham's visit was a waste of time, but he'd gone down fighting.

Because of the thumb injury I badly wanted a warm-up fight, though Pender's crowd were against it. It suited them to keep Pender quiet, because he was old enough not to want too much action. My type of fighting demanded more work. After putting our case a bit strong the Board agreed to an overweight match. I was paired with Canadian champion Wilf Greaves—but the fight never came off. I had to pull out because I felt too weak! I nearly fell over in the gymnasium boxing a welter-weight and an American old-timer Charlie Cotton. Perhaps because of the hand-poisoning injections and being unfit to bear a British winter, I developed a chest infection. I felt like an old man. An X-ray showed my chest was badly congested. So doctors—more of them!—advised me to get away in the sun only eight weeks before I was due to fight Pender. I went to Majorca, and the rest seemed to do the trick.

But, without realizing, it took me almost a year to recover. I was eventually matched again with Pender on April 7, 1962 —nine months after Wembley. It was far too long for me to be out of the ring, without the added worries of illness. The rest suited him more than me.

I felt I'd been out of form for so long that I refused to fly to America, as there had been a tragic New York plane crash. I thought how Frenchman Marcel Cerdan, a world middle-weight champion, had died in a disaster going for a fight in the States. So we booked on the swank *Queen Elizabeth*. I could swim a yard or two—but I couldn't fly an inch. I insisted that Barbara, who was expecting, and Wendy go with me. I realize it sounds as though it's breaking all championship-fight rules, where champ and challenger are supposed to eat rusty nails in log-camp quarters.

I would work like a dog, talk and study boxing until I was blue in the face. But at night I needed a break or I'd drive everyone mad. Barbara didn't mind me driving her mad. And, believe me, when a fight nears, each day gets harder for a woman to bear. But, at least, Barbara understood.

I took my new trainer, Danny Vary, whose accent ain't no improvement on mine, and George Aldridge, who was a good spar-mate and proudly won a fight in Boston. We travelled first-class and I'm telling you it was a sight for sore eyes to see me, Vary, and Aldridge rigged out in dinner jackets.

We looked like three bouncers at a Chicago speak-easy! Tough as they are, Danny and George went a bit green first day out to sea. Cunard Line did me proud when the crew made a gym available for me.

We got a great welcome in America, with Johnny Dunne, my man in Boston, really on the ball. We drove through town in a Cadillac and I revelled in the push-button windows that nearly chopped Vary's head off. We also had another car loaned, quietly emblazoned 'Terry Downes, World Champion'.

I wanted a family life away from the routine of hotel, and Sam Burns had found the ideal spot in Brookline, just around the corner from Pender's home! It was Hampton Court. The Massachusetts Commission asked Pender and me to play it cool, because boxing had just suffered a big blow with the death of world champion Benny Paret after fighting Emil Griffith at Madison Square Garden.

Death in the ring didn't help the nerves, but I never worried. I regard these rare accidents as part-and-parcel of the risks. We moved into the ideal gymnasium, normally reserved for wrestlers, alongside the Boston Arena. I couldn't complain about a thing, except that finding a road-running route was not easy. I'd been stopped from running around a reservoir. Brookline, I may add, is some snooty place.

The set-up was going well and Sam Burns sailed with us to take charge. When two husky characters banged on our suite door, wearing cop-style trilbies and sporting guns and black-jacks, I thought it was a stick-up. I swear Sam turned whiter than a sheet. They turned out to be two smashing fellahs, Bob Hall and Joe Walsh, a coupla fearless detectives from the local station. Those New York cops in the TV series 'Naked City' look like fairies compared with these boys.

They wanted to make sure we weren't being molested, and called around all the time or gave me a ride in their prowl-car —sirens an' all. They were right up Vary's alley, since he knew more about law-breakers than law-abiders. He practically joined the Brookline force. They even put us in an identi-fication parade, threw us in the can, took fingerprints, and really gave us a great laugh. I even got them to 'arrest' Mickey Duff on gambling charges when he arrived.

Bob and Joe were helpful enough to tour me around the road area where Pender had prepared before moving his camp to Manomet, up-state near Plymouth Rock. So I took to the same road as Pender, even passing his dad's house, where I'd give 'em a cheeky nod. Then Johnny Dunne took me around to meet Pender senior, a likable old boy.

The two cops were honest. They were keen Pender supporters and kept telling me he was sure to beat the hell out of me, because Paul's brother Bill was a patrolman at their station.

I was getting fit and just when I considered my luck had turned I came close to having my foot crushed! Reg Gutteridge was the only reporter to witness the near miss and it supplied him with a story. Some weight-lifter barbells were thrown on top of my speed-ball platform to prevent vibration. During a training session a barbell slipped off the platform, grazing my shoulder, and by sheer luck crashed only an inch from my foot. It was my turn to turn white.

But that, luckily, was the only incident to upset my training. I went into the fight without a complaint. I got a nice morale-booster being given a swank reception in the French and Adam suite of the Ritz-Carlton when Nat Fleischer presented me with the *Ring* magazine silver belt. But, just my luck, somebody spoiled the occasion, presenting dear ole Nat with a million-dollar libel writ.

We had the usual disagreement with the Commission and Sam and Waltham told them I definitely wouldn't fight if they chose a certain referee we had good reason to think would favour Pender. But they kept us guessing until fight-time. They appointed James McCarron, a Somerville bank president, and I had no complaint—until after the fight. I claim the ref permitted Pender to get away with daylight robbery by grabbing me whenever I tried to punch. I called it the Boston Grab championship.

When Pender grabbed me like a leech in the first round I deliberately banged me head into him. Rough stuff? Yes, but I had to do something desperate to frighten him from holding. Everything and everybody was against me, and I knew it. I wouldn't have screamed if Pender had butted me right back.

There's nothing that angers me more than knowing an

opponent is holding and thieving a fight. The referee said he'd sling me out if I used the head again. I didn't. But I kept pushing my glove into Pender's bent nose whenever he was holding, in the hope he'd get off a bit quicker. That didn't work, either.

He turned a bit nasty, hitting me with a right-hand punch after the second-round bell ended. Even the locals booed him. The Bostonians were a fair crowd. In the third my left eye was cut, but not enough to bother me. In the next round Pender's left eyebrow was cut, so we were even. In my mind I had definitely won the first five rounds, was boxing well, and, judging from the other fights, I figured Pender could never stand the pace.

But Pender surprised me. His trainer, Al Lacey, was rousing him and practically manhandling him off his stool to start some rounds and if I'd thrown everything at the right time I have a feeling Pender would have quit again. But he was fighting hard to prove himself. The Americans hadn't forgiven him for quitting in London. In the seventh a bit of blood flowed from the side of my nose and I was having trouble breathing—but I hadn't lost any medals. I felt I was still Pender's guv'nor and I was always more aggressive. Without me trying it would have been a stinker of a fight.

In the eighth I fell through the ropes, with Pender falling over me, and crashed my back on the ring apron. I never felt any effect at the time, yet it did a lot to knock the fight out of me. From the ninth to thirteenth rounds I had a bad patch. His left hand was going great and he started to get stronger. I couldn't understand it. Strength was usually my game. I was tiring, had a bad tenth, with my nose bleeding, and Danny and Johnny painted some black healer on my nose to stem the blood.

Trying to disentangle myself at close quarters was making me more tired than Pender, but I was sticking in my share of punches and certainly doing all the inside work. He picked me off pretty good at long range. I reckoned by the thirteenth we were about level, though I was convinced that in England Pender would have been disqualified for holding.

How the last three rounds were scored probably decided the winner. The last round was the best of the fight and we belted away unmercifully, both our faces bruised and bleeding, and refusing to budge an inch. We kept punching after the last bell because neither of us heard the finish with the roar of the crowd. I couldn't stand still while they totted up the score-cards and, though I was not expecting favours, I still thought I'd pinched the points. So did Sam Burns. I realize I couldn't be the greatest judge inside the ring but I felt I'd landed more punches.

But the winner and new champeen, only the fourth middle-weight in history to regain the crown, was Pender. It must have been close. On the Boston ten-point-round system the referee scored 144 to 143 for Pender. Judge Joe Blumsack scored it 145—143 to Pender, and the other one, Harry French —he must have been watching a different fight!—reckoned it 146—141 for Pender. My manager reckoned I'd been refereed out of the fight.

We got back to the dressing-room for the usual inquest and somehow I honestly felt a weight had been lifted off my shoulders. The championship had brought me nothing but trouble. While the hordes of reporters and fight fraternity, which included the retired Peter Waterman who'd made his first trip, were still sorting out the arguments, I stepped into the shower with Pender.

'We've been together all night, Paul, no use breaking it up now,' I said. He laughed and we chatted about our families. We were both banged-up around the face and bruised around the body. Just a coupla honest pro's had finished another night's work. And still an Englishman had not come out of America with a world title. If only I could have delayed the fight a couple of months longer, and taken a ten-rounder for practice, maybe things would have been different. I felt fit enough, but my first and only fifteen rounds proved too much after the illness. Serves me right for keeping my word. Maybe that's why I won't be pushed around by anyone now.

The title did not bring much luck for Pender. He had a car crash and six months later, after he tried unsuccessfully to

M

negotiate a fight with Gene Fullmer, the New York Commission stripped him of the title. That, too, was a diabolical liberty helped by a bit of pressure from the British Board pushing the claims of Dick Tiger. Of course, Tiger deserved his chance. But I disagreed with the way the authorities kicked Pender up the backside. But that's his worry. (Pender, incidentally, is retired and running a Boston bakery.)

Peter Wilson was again pulling no punches with his report, which was headed: 'Quit, Terry! You can only go down now.' Turn it up, Peter. I wasn't counted out or carried out. You couldn't say I'd put up a bad show. There was still plenty of money to be made. Besides, I liked to fight. And there was a big pay-day awaiting, to meet the man I admired more than any fighter—the fabulous Sugar Ray Robinson.

The *Daily Mirror* printed an inquest headed: '*Should that perishin' 'ooter be stuck up for more punishment?*' Their printed letters gave me the verdict 8 to 6. That encouraged me to go on fighting. I've earned £30,000 since then—and more to come!

To add to my misery in Boston—we were no Glee Party—all the English, except Barbara and me, scarpered home while I had to stay on for the court hearing that had been delayed since the writs were issued at the first Pender fight weigh-in. Leavey and Cartier claimed about £18,000 as a percentage due to them for breaking a contract. That was a bit strong for a profit for doing exactly nothing. Although I was right worried about the case, at least I knew it wouldn't cost me much. Jarvis Astaire, like a good 'un, had guaranteed to pay my costs—but I'll bet even he never realized how high they'd go.

A New York lawyer, Herman Levene—no relation of Harry's but an uncle of Jarvis's—always considered my Baltimore contract was not valid. In the Superior Court in Equity, of Suffolk, Massachusetts, the battle (Case No. 77752) began. Talk about TV's Perry Mason and Sam Benedict. They weren't in it with our legal mob. I called up a heavy-weight Boston lawyer, James Lynch, who stood 6 ft. 3 in., while Cartier and Leavey, besides having Vincent Cartier in their corner, had another big geezer, Tom McNearney, a local criminal lawyer. If you ain't heard two Boston Irishmen battling you ain't heard nothing. Boy, did they have a Donnybrook battle!

The hearing was fixed for one day. It went on longer. After the first round I thought my chances were 50—1 against winning. They made me sound like a real criminal. But my geezer went fighting back. In the end, with me sweating a bit, Justice Thomas J. Spring, bless him, declared me a complete winner.

He summed up:

'I find that Downes at the time of his signing of the contract was twenty (20) years of age, having been born on May 9, 1936.

'I find that the contract entered into by Downes was voidable at his option, he being an infant at the time of his signing the contract.

'I find that at no time did Downes ratify or confirm this contract.

'I find that Downes' failure to return to the U.S.A. until December 1960 was sufficient evidence of Downes' intention to disaffirm or avoid the contract.

'I find that Downes' disaffirmance of this contract was made within a reasonable time after he attained his majority.

'I find that the signature of Downes' parents on the contract cannot defeat Downes' right of disaffirmance.

'I find that Leavey had never been licensed as manager of boxers until January 1959, when he made application and received a licence to manage Downes in the State of Maryland.

'I find that Cartier had never been licensed to manage boxers until 1960 when he applied for and was granted a licence to manage Downes by the State of Maryland.

'I find that neither Cartier nor Leavey made any application for a licence to manage Downes in any other State except in the State of Maryland.

'I find that Cartier never applied for a licence to manage Downes until he realized that Downes had become a successful boxer.

M*

'I find that the five hundred dollars ($500.00) check given Downes by Vincent Cartier on Sunday, December 9, 1956, was merely a goodwill gesture on the part of Cartier to Downes.

'I find that on two occasions Downes or a person acting in his behalf attempted to return the five hundred dollars ($500.00) but Cartier refused to accept it.

'I find that neither Cartier nor Leavey at any time contacted or attempted to contact Downes for the purposes of having him live up to the terms of his contract until this suit was commenced.

'I find that Cartier never spoke to or contacted Downes in any way after their visit in New York City in October or November 1956.

'I find that at no time did Leavey discuss with Downes' parents or sister the question as to when Downes was returning to the U.S.A.

'I find that neither Cartier nor Leavey made any effort to procure a boxing engagement in behalf of Downes during the period the contract was to have been in effect.

'I find that the contract being in the form of boxer-manager agreement, there is no agreement on the part of Richard Downes for which he can be charged.

ORDER

'It is hereby ordered that a decree be entered dismissing the plaintiffs' bill of complaint and awarding the defendants their costs.

'Signed: Thomas J. Spring
Justice of the Superior Court.'

Those last few words 'awarding the defendants their costs' ain't exactly a winner because in America the costs granted are just nominal. When I had a call-over, later, with Astaire, defending the case had cost him £2,000. Like I said before, it's no use having a second-rater for a manager when you're fighting in the big leagues of America. So I'd got the cut hooter and he'd taken the cut in the pocket. We were a right gruesome twosome. . . .

I sailed back from the States—back in training. I'd gone there doing my road-work around the main decks and was tuning-up on the way home to fight Don Fullmer, of Utah, brother of Gene. I was back, top of the Wembley bill, forty-five days after losing to Pender.

While training for Fullmer I worked in a betting-shop on my twenty-sixth birthday—and will never forget it. A geezer came in and laid down £1,000 in single notes and backed a horse called Ann Boleyn at 5—2 on. It won. I wished the punter a successful come-back.

The fight with Fullmer was a bad one. He was a hard little guy who ducked and dived, and I had to go looking for him. It didn't suit my style and, to top it up, I busted my left-hand knuckle early in the fight. Never mind, I won the ten-round points well enough and wasn't marked. But both manager and trainer still reckoned I hadn't fully recovered from the chest trouble that had weakened me. They were right.

So the match I had always sought—me against Sugar Ray—was postponed from July to September 25, 1962—the same night that Sonny Liston pulverized Floyd Patterson in Chicago.

But, need I say, I was sorting out the top specialists, to hell with the expense, to figure out why I'd fought badly against Fullmer. My sore knuckle turned out to be a small but clean break and was treated by Sir Reginald Watson-Jones, consultant to the Queen. Nothing but the best for Her Majesty and me.

His Sirship said I'd have to test the hand the hard way—punching a bag. The first whacks came through without a pain, so we sent for Sugar Ray.

But again there was more heartache in store. Something tougher to take than personal pain. Barbara weighed-in with our second baby in June 1962. It looked so pugnacious we had to call it Terry junior! But the poor little blighter's lungs collapsed and for two weeks he was kept in an incubator. We were told he had just a 50—50 chance to survive. Barbara and me sweated. After losing her previous baby this was tough to take. And we knew that little Terry's life was in the lap of the gods. The late President Kennedy and his wife lost their child with a similar lung complaint.

Happily, Terry turned out to be something like his old man —a fighter. He pulled through and has the stoutest pair of lungs you've ever heard. So I was able to condition myself both physically and mentally for Sugar Ray.

I had watched Robinson while I was in the States and say without hesitation that he is the greatest fighter I've ever seen. I say he's the best at any weight in history. You may kid yourself that's smart flattery from me because I went on to outpoint Robinson at Wembley, which would make me even greater. Just like Gene Tunney always says Jack Dempsey was the greatest—because he beat him twice!

I've got news for you. It would be a liberty to say I beat Robinson. Yes, I won without doubt, I think, but nobody has ever heard me claim I beat *the* Sugar Ray. The name was the same, but I beat a forty-one-year-old man going through the motions from memory. At twenty-five, as a welter-weight, Robinson was fantastic. That was the man I'd have liked to have beaten. But just being associated with his name, sharing the same ring, and providing a smashing fight for a complete sell-out crowd—not to mention the £9,000 I got—gave me more satisfaction than winning a world title. I mean that. I looked up to Robinson, although I know he isn't liked by most of the fight fraternity in America. He had everything I admire in a fighter.

We met at a Park Lane reception, dolled up like millionaires, and despite a few know-alls saying we were both over the hill, you couldn't buy a ticket a week before the fight. Robinson was magic and the crowd knew, at least, I'd always give them value. Touts got £25 for a £6 ticket.

Did I say over the hill? Only seven months before fighting me Robinson had k.o.'d Wilf Greaves, who held a verdict over Dick Tiger for the Empire title and who had drawn in London with Mick Leahy, later to become British champion. And for eighteen months after Robinson fought me he lost only one of twelve fights—on points to world champion Giardello!

I brought trainer Johnny Dunne over from Boston because he knew Robinson's style. He ordered me to keep pushing Robinson back because Ray wanted room to work. I couldn't change my fight-pattern late in life and expect to outbox him. The one thing I wouldn't allow was Ray's terrific flurries of punches when backed up to the ropes. I'd seen his hair stand on end throwing these punches and he'd made me ooze with admiration. So I pressed Ray too close, just throwing some soft punches to keep him occupied.

They say they gave him whiffs of oxygen in the corner and they must have stuck a horseshoe in his glove around the fifth round. He wobbled me with a peach of a left hook. But I refused to stop pressing and forcing him to fight the full three minutes of every round. I just wore him down.

I'd watch Ray half smiling and throwing his combination punches and trying to kid me he was still fresh. I knew he had to be tiring and thought I fought a smart fight kidding him right back. This was a fight I really enjoyed.

Don't tell Harry Levene, but I'd have fought Robinson for expenses only, for the privilege of being in there with him. Sugar came out for the last round with a wonderful grandstand finish. He whipped punches at me and I thought, 'Gawd, what must this geezer have been like fifteen years ago?' But the flash only lasted about half a minute and I got back into the fight again.

Referee Andy Smyth, whose presence made the night perfect for me, hoisted my hand and Robinson's handler, George Gainford, looked disgusted and made the usual protest. But there was never really any doubt about the verdict. Dear old Bill McGowran wrote that Robinson, whatever the hysteria, had only won one round and shared a couple.

The crowd were calling for a return of a fight many reckoned had proved the Fight of the Year. It's a night I'll always cherish in my memory. And I regret that a TV film was not made of the fight.

Ray and I frequently bumped into each other when we were both training at the same gym in London for further fights. The man was a charmer, like a film-star. We'd chat away like old pals. It's surprising how friendly fighters can be, despite the rough stuff of the ring.

Because I kept in constant training I picked up another

£7,000 for a nice healthy exercise fighting Phil Moyer, of Oregon, whom we called Phil the Pill-Boxer. He came here with a suitcase loaded with various vitamin pills. A punch up the belly and I had him shaking like a rattle.

It was a lucky fight for me because Henry Cooper was booked to fight Dick Richardson, but knocked up his elbow. I went in against Moyer as a save-the-show substitute. It was a tasty pick-up. The fight? He'd beaten guys like Don Fullmer and Don Jordan, but he never gave me much bother. I won in nine rounds, but with blood dripping down my neck from a cut on the head.

It coincided with me forfeiting my British title. A few hours after stopping Moyer I was *ex*-British champion without throwing a punch. . . .

Why I Fight

Losing the title out of the ring was no joke. And I'll tell you exactly how it happened. It caused such a hullabaloo at the time and there was so much stupidly wrong opinion that I'm pleased, at last, to explain. According to rule I forfeited the title by refusing to meet the nominated challenger. So I'm not bitching about that.

In fact I'll never cry if I don't fight for a national title again. They can keep British titles, because the Board become the watchdog, often decide purse-money, and dictate too much. There's no real privilege being champion, though I have admitted that I was real proud when I first won the title.

The Board had nominated John McCormack for a third fight with me. Admitted, at the time he was the only real challenger, but I still didn't think he deserved the chance after our two bloody and lousy fights.

Between the fights with Ray Robinson and Phil Moyer we were busy trying to make a deal with Gene Fullmer, and I had Los Angeles promoter George Parnassus pulling for me. There was a fair chance of the fight coming off. It meant a big pay-day and, with Paul Pender under suspension, we might also have fought for the world title. I figured Fullmer was ready to be taken. I turned out right about that, too.

There were also negotiations going on for a return with Robinson, which would have brought me at least £10,000. But the Board decided they wanted to keep the championship moving, and nominated McCormack, though for the life of me I couldn't see this as a fight the public cared about. It wasn't as though I was ducking somebody I was scared of. I'd virtually whipped him twice, if you ignore the disqualification after I decked him ten times!

I told Sam Burns to write to the Board explaining that because we had so many other promises I didn't want to spoil my chances of another world-title fight by being committed to meet McCormack again. I told the Board that I did not intend to fight McCormack before they sent out notices to promoters that they would accept purse-offer bids.

I'd remembered all the cuts and troubles—including poor pay—I'd got with McCormack twice before. I knew I couldn't look good defeating him. He's the type who might always make me look bad. As a professional, I had to think of these angles. I didn't want to hand-pick any opponents—God forbid, I'm not scared of anybody—but I resented having to share my purse-money to help make McCormack rich. He'd get 40 per cent of the total.

I knew when I told Burns to write the letter to the Board that I was liable to lose my title. Although McCormack was bugging me, I would not have agreed to defend against anyone else at that time. I didn't want to be tied up.

But the Board ignored my notice and duly sent out for purse offers, which remain sealed until a set date. Another thing that annoyed me was the timing. Only one major promoter had a date booked to be able to bid for the fight. Jack Solomons' offer of £8,600 was accepted by the Board. Champion and challenger split 60—40 per cent, which is another practice I think is scandalous. A champion is entitled to a much bigger share, even though in some cases the challenger could be the better box-office draw.

My whack would be £5,160, a fair pay-day but still less than I earned for a meaningless fight the same month with Phil Moyer. Because Solomons had 'won' the fight the gossip-mongers—their opinions are not worth two bob—said it was backstage needle and I was refusing to fight for Solomons.

That's a load of rubbish. I'll take anyone's money. Besides, I've never had a bad word with Solomons. I was billed to meet McCormack at Wembley on November 27, though the contracts were never signed. Naturally, Solomons shouted in the Press and threatened to sue me for damages and all sorts of pressures came for me to go through with the fight. But no damages were ever claimed. I'm a stubborn geezer and admit it. This attitude, if anything, only made me more determined *not* to fight. Solomons told the newspapers he was willing to give the fight away for Levene to promote. It made a good laugh. He had nothing to give away. The choice of promoters didn't enter into it. We had told the Board of my decision before personalities were introduced.

Let's make it clear that although general opinion has always been that the Board stripped me of my title, in fact they never did. I gave it up. And the Stewards of Appeal (the House of Lords of the Boxing Board) confirmed the Board had no right to sit in judgement once I had informed them of my decision not to defend. The dethroning was automatic.

So ex-champion Downes saw McCormack matched with his old spar-mate, George Aldridge, for the vacant title at Belle Vue, Manchester. George won—and good luck to him—but it was a shocking fight. McCormack practically folded up and has never since fought as a middle-weight. To rub it in, the Board pressed Aldridge's claims for a European title match with Laszlo Papp, the old Hungarian who won three Olympic Gold Medals. If the Board were trying to impress me they failed. They didn't do Aldridge any favours. I doubt if an Aldridge versus Papp match would have been allowed if George hadn't got the title tag. You can't make a different fighter overnight. Poor old George took a right whacking from Papp in Vienna and never really recovered from the fight. He lost the British title in one round and retired early in 1964.

I know that boxing must be regulated. I know that without the Board of Control, who are probably better than most other bodies, the game wouldn't last five minutes. But I personally can't say the Board have done much for me. Let's put a few things right. My first three fights for the world championship were all negotiated by my managers, though, naturally, the Board were involved with official letters after the deals were done.

Although the Board took around £2,000 'cut' from my purse

and film-rights, etc., of the fight with Pender at Wembley in 1961 they would not send an official representative to act as helper for the third match with Pender in America. I repeat, I paid the bulk of the fare for the secretary, Teddy Waltham, to be there.

I've also discussed earlier the diabolical matter of Pender demanding extra use of hand-bandaging at Wembley and the Board bowing to him. I just don't like the way they work. Their attitude, I think, gets a bit too pompous. I'm no rebel. I've worked hard and tried to fight fair and give value in the ring. I don't really dislike the Board of Control. But I feel absolutely nothing for them. I don't like the idea of a champion being told to do this and that and for how much.

I doubt if the public realizes that the Board have virtually got a handful of top fighters providing much of the money to run the Board. They must look around at fighters like me, Henry Cooper, Dave Charnley, Howard Winstone, Brian Curvis, and Billy Walker, and say 'that's our little team'.

The Board deduct 5 per cent after expenses (it's virtually 4 per cent) of the two highest-paid boxers of a bill that exceeds £2,500, or when they earn £500 or more. It's a steady rake-off for them. But it becomes a bit of a blow having these niggly 'cuts' added to the 25 per cent due to managers and some for trainers, when, like me, you don't consider the Board are doing enough. This fighting game is a tough game, mate, and nobody looks out for us when we're finished.

The earning period is only a few years and I reckon such deductions are a liberty. The Board also cop very nicely getting a booking fee the moment they O.K. a date for television. That's fair enough, but they also take 10 per cent of the fee settled with the TV company by the promoter. So that's a bit more out of our end of the money. And, don't forget, we pay boxing-licence fees. It would be fairer to raise them. I know the Board must have money to survive and I appreciate that the Stewards are honourable and unpaid and that Secretary Waltham has an unenviable and, maybe, underpaid job. But let them promote a show or take other measures to make money. I'm fed-up with this milking.

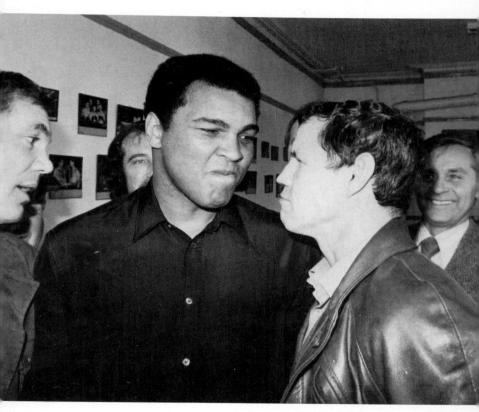

Trying to out-growl Ali, 1972

With Ray Clarke, President of the Board of Control *(left)*,
and Bernard Hart of Lonsdale Sports, 1976

A Variety Club lunch at the Guildhall, with the Duchess of Kent, in 1985

With Paul and Terry Junior in 1985

Willie Pastrano and I, in 1987, remember our last fight

My grandchildren, Jamie and Charlie

My youngest son Richard's
twenty-first birthday

At a Variety Club race meeting at Sandown Park in 1986,
with Barbara and grandson, Jamie

I also disagreed with the Board's action in April 1964, withdrawing from the European Boxing Union without any warning or backing of the licence-holders. Such a big decision should surely have been discussed by the various area councils at the Board's A.G.M. They say Britain's withdrawal from the E.B.U. will not affect British boxers' chances of winning titles. I don't believe it.

Among the Board's reasons for withdrawal, according to their own letter in the trade paper, was because the E.B.U. was 'principally interested in amateur boxing and, in consequence, professional boxers and their particular problems have taken second place'.

If the Board were so concerned with pro boxing they have hit their own boxers where it hurts most—in the pocket. Less chances of boxing for Eurpoean titles means less earning. A lot of British boxers, with Dick Richardson a prime example, grabbed a fortune with E.B.U. titles. I'll bet Dick would admit he copped around £60,000 without even having a European fight in England.

It's all right for the Board to worry about their principles. We've got to worry about our money. And I don't like the idea of our Board backing out just because they couldn't get their own way. At least we had some chance of straightening things out while Britain was represented. Now we're on the outside looking in. And I'm speaking without personal bias because I never fought for the European title—and now never will.

There's also a lot of argument about fights being in the hands of one referee, our system, or with a vote from two judges and a referee. I'm strongly in favour of referee and judges. It's nothing against British referees, because they're as good as any, and better than most. But I've always believed a referee handling a hard fight has enough on his hands without the sole responsibility of scoring.

I also think there can be too much at stake for one man to make a mistake with a bad decision. I know judges also come up with their share of bad verdicts, especially the amateurs, but it's my conviction that a mistake is less likely to happen with three votes than one. Also, I consider what I know as unconscious bias by a referee. He reads about a boxer having a wonderful left hand and maybe without realizing it the referee scores points automatically for this punch even when the punch isn't really deserving of points. See what I mean?

I'm also convinced certain referees 'favour' certain styles. Plenty of ringsiders in London pick out refs who like left-hand-boxer types; others who favour aggressive fighters. It's also too much to expect an inexperienced ref to spot a crafty fighter holding on the blind side and hitting. And whenever the crowd go home shouting that a referee is 'fixed'—and that, honestly, is the last thing I'd ever accuse any British referee of—I think it would be fairer to everyone if we had judges. At least a crowd couldn't accuse all of them of being biased, bent, or call it what you like. But don't let's blind ourselves. Some of the public—and trade people who should know better—do accuse a ref of being bribed!

I often think the Board are at fault paying most of their attention to rights and wrongs at big shows because they're afraid of the publicity it will bring. Anything to keep the peace. It's the small shows, where some of the more tender kids can get hurt, that should be watched. A lot of the worst decisions take place in small halls with small fights, but nobody seems to care. It's all wrong.

But considering all the 'bad' publicity boxing gets—and most of it is stirred up by people who get their living from the game—I consider it a straight game. I owe a lot to boxing, and I love it. Yes, I actually *care* about the game.

As for fighters 'throwing' a fight, you can forget that in this country—as I have said earlier in the book. I think the writers and authorities would be better off worrying about football and horse-racing, where fixing has been *proved* to take place. O.K., so boxing often attracts a lot of layabouts. But it also turns a few layabouts into respectable geezers. At least the blood we fighters spill is honest.

Talking of blood reminds me I haven't shed so much lately. I haven't drawn much from the blood bank for a long time. I had a nice nine-and-a-half-round exercise against American Jimmy Beecham in a live TV fight in March, 1963, for a £4,000 pay-out. I'd been out of the ring four months because

my mind was more occupied, and worried, about the serious
illness of my dad. If I can't concentrate on training I can't
fight. So some of the critics had a go at me for making hard
work of Beecham.

The way I punched I'd have had trouble putting my old
woman down for the full count and since Beecham had been a
trialhorse for better whackers than me I wasn't taking daft risks
and busting my hands. Beecham hadn't exactly been knocking
over any trees, but nobody knocks him over. With tension
off, and not trying to look good or worry about titles, I thought
I'd boxed relaxed and well enough.

I was 'wanted' by several promoters, despite the modest
reviews, but because of Dad's illness I was out of action for
seven months. He couldn't stand the strain of knowing I was
fighting while he was helpless. I confess that during the spring
of 1963 I came closest to quitting the game. When Dad was
weakening he made a plea to me to pack up. How could I
refuse?

The thought of packing in while I was still physically in my
prime was heartbreaking. Watching Dad fading was far worse.
I confess I cracked under the strain and cried, unashamedly,
on Sam Burns' shoulder.

But, as Rocky Graziano used to say, 'Somebody up there
likes me'. Dad made a marvellous come-back by responding to
ray treatment. With him brighter, though still cheating with
time, I began training and he came to the gym to watch me. It
was like old times. Gradually, he encouraged me and I felt the
old urge to begin punching again. Fighting is my life. I decided to fight, for the first time, as a cruiser-weight (limit
12 st. 7 lb.), and though I admit that for the first time in my
life I was not 100 per cent trained I came back to knock over
Rudolph Nehring, my first German rival, at the Albert Hall.
He was no trouble—out in two rounds.

For my forty-first fight I took on American Mike Pusateri,
from Brockton, Mass., at Belle Vue, Manchester, where Levene
was going great guns. Pusateri, a rough and game guy, had
Rocky Marciano, the old heavy-weight champion, shouting for
him. Rocky was there to support him because his old trainer,

Allie Colombo, managed Mike. We had a fair old punch-up, but, in better shape, I boxed above myself. Mike suited me fine. I wore him down in five rounds—and gratefully got rave notices.

But, behind the scenes, Jarvis Astaire and Barbara were battling with their conscience. The night before the fight Jarvis had received a telephone call from Baltimore, passed on by frantic sister, Sylvie, who was looking after Dad for a few weeks. We felt a change of scenery and getting him away from English fog would buck him up.

Dad had taken a turn for the worse. Sylvie wanted me to fly across the Atlantic right away. Jarvis felt this was a family decision and consulted Barbara. She felt I must go through with the fight—and they decided not to say anything until afterwards. Despite the excitement of the victory I left Belle Vue despondent. They broke the bad news and I thanked Jarvis for sensibly holding it back until I'd finished my fight.

Without hardly having the chance to read the fight reports I was boarding a plane for America for what seemed the longest nine-odd hours of my life. Would I make it in time? Fortunately I did, and somehow the tonic of my presence and, maybe, the win helped revive Dad. Despite the worry of how he would react to jet flying, I brought him home again.

My Dad, bless him, did not live to enjoy the chat of this story. He'd read much of the transcript, laughed at the ribbing I was giving him, and like a good father backed me in all of the opinions. He died in the summer of 1964, at fifty-four. He suffered to the end with cancer and, typical of him, overstayed his expected life by a couple of years. What a great battler he was. I was very proud of my old man. I miss him greatly. I have the consolation of knowing that he, at least, shared in some of my successes and that I tried to be a good son.

My sister flew from Baltimore when we knew Dad couldn't beat the count and we were together, with Mum, at the end. Sylvie had to rush home to care for her children—but tragedy struck again. Within a week of Dad's funeral Sylvie's two-year-old daughter had fallen into a garden plastic swimming-pool and drowned. This was worse than any beatings I'd taken in the ring. Mum had gone to recuperate in Somerset and I rushed to break the bad news. We were airborne within a few hours without a bag packed between us. Again she was on her way to face a second tragedy in Baltimore. Sylvie was consoled with our presence. She took this terrible blow most bravely.

I went over the Border to Scotland for the first time in 1964 for a TV fight at the Kelvin Hall, Glasgow. Peter Keenan, ex-bantam champion whom I reckoned a real pro, was the promoter. I was matched against Ed Zaremba, a right hard nut from Jacksonville, Michigan. Zaremba might have always been last to be called at school but he made his name against me. I'd been out for seven months and was a bit rusty. It took me a few rounds to work back into real shape. I tagged Ed a corker right in the first which made him buckle, clutch and wrestle to save himself. When I couldn't dump him down again I resigned myself to staying the ten rounds—especially when I'd sprained a thumb in the fourth round. I had Zaremba rocking and reeling in the last and was pleased with the way I pulled out the stops. But he survived and I was first to lead the applause. I'd taken the points without any argument, but what a game guy!

It's the first time on record that a Limey has put both the American boxer and manager in the same hospital at the same time. Harry Baxter, sixty-one, Scottish-born but domiciled in Detroit for thirty years, collapsed before the fight and was taken for treatment. Ed went for a check-up for a pulled muscle and busted rib. I didn't escape without a scratch. I fought covered with blood—but not mine for a change. Then a butt by Zaremba brought a 3 in. gash on the crown of my head.

The three cruiser-weight battles had given me a No. 6 rating with the World Boxing Association. I began feeling on top of the world again. Sam Burns, taking a combined business-pleasure holiday in Miami, Florida, talked terms with Willie Pastrano to defend his world championship against me. Mickey Duff, who did a feat by officially promoting in Omaha, Nebraska, also flew to Miami—the locals call it My-am-ah—on behalf of Harry Levene. Jarvis Astaire kept the trans-Atlantic phones buzzing. Between them they pulled it off—

Pastrano v. Downes for the world title at Manchester, November 30, 1964—after Willie sought a postponement from a September date. Could I become the first Englishman to win *two* world titles at two different weights? It wouldn't be for the lack of trying!

The between-fight periods were busily filled with keeping an eye on the business interests. I bought a house at Mill Hill, Middlesex, with a swimming-pool and a few acres of ground which meant I could do my road-work without leaving home! It was a long way from those hard days at Paddington—but I was still around with the same boys. I also turned out for several charity football matches, from Leyton Orient to Cardiff grounds. As they say, I got a kick out of it. Some of my mates had fun organizing a London to Brighton walk—pushing a fruit barrow! We decided to jib-in—that means intrude—on the London market porters' annual charity race. We loaded up with the regulation 1 cwt and began at midnight. I'm ashamed to admit that my 'plates of meat' started swelling by the time we'd passed through Croydon, Surrey—about fifteen miles— and I couldn't go on in stockinged feet.

But one of my sparring-partners, Lennie (Legs) Cain, of Notting Hill, and Georgie (Fainting) Smith, of Islington, kept the team barrow going and finished the course. Can you imagine how tough that is? Those of us who swallowed it presented the game guys with cups.

Sam Burns, whose teenage years were spent writing racing for *The Sporting Life* and the *Evening News*, became a racehorse owner—and called the animal Terry Downes. We got top-jockey Lester Piggott to ride him at Ascot. But after Terry Downes' first three races he still hadn't won. It ran more like Sam Burns than me.

You wonder why I go on boxing? I've got money for life, but so have Paul Getty and Charlie Clore. They still enjoy working. My work is harder, but I'm potty enough to enjoy it, too. I don't earn a penny from the ring. All the money I collect from the ring goes into trust for my three kids—Wendy, Terry, and Paul.

I can't think of a better reason for a man to fight.

The Last Hurrah

I T was fitting, as it turned out, to finish the hardback version of this book on the eve of fighting again for the championship of the world in 1964. This time moving up to light heavy-weight. My old rival, Dick Tiger, had won the two titles only, sadly, to die later with a broken spirit after the terrible Nigeria-Biafra war.

It seemed I was going to be messed about in the middle-weight division. The openings weren't easy, like today, with more weights available. Straw-weight to super-weight and all that. Some would have been lucky to be champion of my street.

I knew I was never a genuine light heavy, but Willie Pastrano, the champion, didn't seem the most devastating puncher, however, as I discovered, he knew the business. They called him Willie the Wisp. He was launched by Angelo Dundee and his cagey brother Chris, as an Italian so that he would become a box-office draw. Years later, Reg Gutteridge revealed, Willie didn't have even a splash of Italian blood though his appearance made him look more 'raddy' than Mussolini. He even went to evening class to learn to speak Italian. He came from Hawaiian-Cajun stock. And a decent bloke too. In 1956, Pastrano was then a star, he refereed a fight of mine when I served with the U.S. Marines.

Angelo regarded Britain as a klondike. Pastrano fought here seven times before he won the light heavy title against Harold Johnson in 1963. I was pleased about that. Not being a big light heavy I think Johnson, a great boxer, might have punched holes in me. But Pastrano outsmarted him.

I saw all but one of Pastrano's fights here. He boxed rings around a full-blown heavy-weight and hard nut, Dick Richardson, with a showing that had them applauding in the aisles at Harringay Arena. He came back to do likewise against another heavy pair, Brian London and Joe Bygraves. But they were like big kippers. Later London won with Pastrano cut in five rounds, a decision that displeased Dundee, known for his skilled blood-stopping in the corner.

But Pastrano couldn't argue when he went on to fight—or box in this case—against Joe Erskine. The Welshman won in a canter. It was time for Willie to count his pound notes and forget about the bigger guys. Had Erskine worked harder at the game I swear he'd still be champion. He knew more strokes than Steve Davis. Honest, Frank Bruno would have had trouble hitting him with a bag of rice.

Competing at his best weight Pastrano, and especially Dundee, couldn't get here quickly enough to defend the title. He stopped Greg Peralta in April 1964 in New Orleans—the champ's hometown—and signed to fight me at the now demolished Kings Hall, Belle Vue, Manchester, on November 30, 1964.

Dundee, of course, knew my style. Willie even had the chance to check up by reading this book hours before the first bell. There's no sentiment in the fight game. Bookies made Pastrano 9–4 favourite. He weighed a quarter pound inside 12st 7lb. I was 12st 3lb soaking wet. I reckoned he had weight-making trouble. The fight became the first to be relayed city-to-city on closed-circuit TV, from Manchester to a London West End theatre.

David Coleman did the commentary, the only one I recall him doing on boxing. The place was packed. It was a great atmosphere hall. It wasn't exactly Paddington Station but I could regard it as 'home'. Trouble was Pastrano was a good traveller, good temperament. He won in Italy and South Africa. The jocks did him, though. Chic Calderwood, another of the champs of my time to die tragically, nicked a points decision in Glasgow.

There were no judges appointed at that time. Sole decision

by the referee. Pastrano had no worries. He trusted British officials, though I'd often said that it was known for British refs to try and show how game they are by giving a close verdict to a foreigner. It doesn't happen in any other country, but decisions in title fights are now taken out of the referee's hands.

The Board of Control's appointment of Andrew Smyth, from Belfast, seemed perfect. I couldn't have hand picked a better ref. Getting on a bit, but always worked a fight well.

I can truthfully say I'd never felt better or more confident. I knew the risks of moving up a weight, but Pastrano looked fast against heavy-weights. How would he cope with a puffed up middle-weight? I didn't spring around the ring but had fast hands and thought. I studied him. Boxing was my business. I always worked at it.

They thought Joey Giardello was going to be too smart and durable for me but I did him at his own game. Even now I don't really get the credit for that win. Giardello had a great record. He fought the best. And I beat him before he dethroned Dick Tiger for the world title.

Anyway, the chance of winning titles at two weights, a bit of a feat during my time, spurred me on. I couldn't believe the start of the fight. I was the one doing the clever bits and Pastrano looked on. A bit of blood appeared high on the head in the first round. I thought hello, 'ere we go again and, though the guy who is cut is always the last to know whether it's bad or not, I knew I had worse cuts shaving. They soon patched it up in the corner.

I made up my mind to chase and harass Pastrano. It worked. His feet were not faster than mine. He seemed confused. Sure he had some successes, why not, but as the fight went along I was certain of winning. This was not the Pastrano who controlled the fight as against Richardson, London & Co. Only because I wouldn't let him.

By the fifth, the crowd knew I could do it. They began chanting my name. It was a wonderful gee for me. Honestly, nothing could go wrong. I gritted teeth and kept charging in, not allowing Pastrano room to manoeuvre. The weight difference was barely noticeable. I felt I could fight all night. In fact, a few pounds over the middle-weight limit seemed to suit me.

Between rounds I could hear Dundee and Lou Gross barking at Pastrano. They knew, as I did, the title was going to change. The longer the fight went, the louder the chants.

But, like they say, it's a funny old game. At the start of the eleventh round, Dundee really whacked Pastrano's rump as he came off the stool.

It makes a good story to say it changed the course of the fight. What really happened was Pastrano threw a right-hand punch intended to catch me—and it did. They say lucky punch. Not at all. He threw it to hit me and it did. Nothing lucky about that. I was stunned and went down. I was pro enough to let the head clear a bit. I was hurt, but not enough to stay down. Pastrano had thrown the punch with such force that he stepped right over me as I went down. Like barging through a door.

But I knew when I got up that Pastrano would come on strong. He was desperate. So when he came at me I immediately considered stalling for a bit of time. I could easily have clutched but deliberately went down on one knee. It seemed the sensible thing to do. I was hurt the first time but not the second. He threw plenty of right handers but he never actually knocked me down. Usually fighters are patted on the back for getting out of trouble taking a count on one knee.

Then, to my surprise and I think everyone else's, Mr. Smyth stopped the fight! I got up and fell back in amazement. I'd seen preliminary fighters take far more stick and allowed to go on. It was so out-of-character for this referee. Years later I'm still bemused by that decision. I've had top officials, even the then New York Commissioner, General Krulewitch, watch the film and say the fight should not have been stopped.

But I never held any grudge against the referee. He did his job as he saw it. Maybe he did me a favour. Had I won—and I would—Harold Johnson was waiting in the wings and he might have half killed me.

It so happens Andrew Smyth retired from the game before I did. I'd made up my mind within minutes of the end that I'd

given all. It was time to go. Nobody had to tell me but we
waited until the following February before calling a press conference at the London Hilton, can't beat a bit of style, when the
writers thought I was announcing another fight. Liked a bit of
mischief. Still do. I waved goodbye.

It was my best fight against Pastrano. Nothing could follow
it.

ROUND 14

Life Is for Living

I NEVER had withdrawal symptoms. You work hard, take the share of stick, revel in a bit of glory, count the money and hang up the gloves. Yet I always feel a part of the fight game. It was what I did best. The ring was my stage. But no way was I going to hang around to become a has-been. Other than winning a world title, fighting for it ('A Gallant Failure' head-lined *Boxing News)* was the highest way to go out.

Mind you, I still had Willie Pastrano to contend with. The Variety Club invited him and me to Manchester in 1986 to celebrate the 20-year-plus anniversary of the fight to raise a nice few quid for children's charities. I'd enjoyed working for the Variety Club and roaming the country, helping raise cash for the Sunshine Coaches. They transport the sick and needy to the beaches that become a vital part of a children's home.

Willie missed the intended plane from New Orleans. Truth was he was struggling for cash and was unable to pay the bits and pieces at the airport. Our lives had gone different ways. He battled against drugs and divorce. The void after boxing was more than Willie could handle. It's understandable. But the old champ, looking portly but still striking, really had a ball here.

We kept him longer than intended, bunged him a few quid, we talked it up, and he made a comeback in life. The Louisiana Boxing Commission enrolled him. But he still fanc-ied coming here and, hopefully, opening a restuarant with me. He'd even found a name. Neutral Corner.

It all sounded lovely, but I'd lost no marbles and wasn't too excited about bank rolling a restaurant. Drink up, have a gig-gle, and go home, Willie.

204

They say the ring is the loneliest place of all. When the bell
goes you're on your own. I appreciated helpers but never
tolerated hangers-on. I'd succeeded without being carried.

I owned property during the ring days. I might sound a bit
of a mumbler at times but I always spoke like it! When it came
to having brains dished out I wasn't exactly at the back of the
queue. Common sense and street smart. You don't have to get
a degree to make it in life but I now admit it helps. A bit of
honesty goes a long way, too.

Anyone who gets a bit of success is often branded as having
'somebody behind them'. Yes, I had a gee from Jarvis Astaire
and Sam Burns and once had substantial shares in the Wil-
liam Hill organization. I was pleased about it. I still have
some. But everything else I did alone.

Property increased in London but it's a right fight a week
trying to collect rent. I seem to have tenants taught by the
Artful Dodger. None the less, it's an income.

I took out a boxers' manager licence, still pay £50 to keep
the Board of Control happy, but have not been connected for
some years. I learned the hard way that the boxers I signed
were not prepared to give the game the same dedication as I
had. I couldn't understand that. I had two useful performers,
Tommy and George Gray. We won fights in South Africa and
Australia. I got them jobs, accommodation, living with my
Mum, and was prepared to be either on the road or in the gym
with them every day. A lot of managers are booking agents.
They pick up a phone and ask how things are going.

I was prepared to get involved. I was never going to make
serious money but the belief that I could mould a good fighter,
especially a champion, was my drive.

Johnny Dunn, the wise old owl who helped train me in Boston during my title days, sent a smart boxer, Dick Ekland, for
me to whip into shape. Ekland had gone ten rounds with
Sugar Ray Leonard. That's talent. Next thing I know he
brings a pal to Britain, I'm always putting my hand in my
pocket, and he's getting homesick. He turned out like others.

Make arrangements for training they turn up an hour late.
They want baby sitting. It seems a modern trend. I'd spent

enough 'sponsoring' and since I've never been accused of
mincing words I said my piece and the sugar daddy days were
over. I still keep the licence just in case the right kid comes
along.

I went back to attending shows and doing most of the hol-
lering and hooting. Listen, life is too serious to be taken
seriously. I paid my dues and bled with the best of them so
I'm entitled to be noisy. It's all harmless, though I daresay
misinterpreted by those not accustomed to the Downes treatment.

To say that I spend a lot of my time raising cash for charities makes me sound like a Father Christmas. But it's something I want to do. I've got a little place at Canvey Island in
Essex where I send the occasional needy old couple for a
break.

Because the Variety Club had plenty of help I was pleased
to be invited as a Lord's Taverner and perform regularly for
their fund raising. Until recently I played a part on the Committee of the Uppercut Club raising funds.

The only non-charitable event is being Captain of the Boxers Golf Society. I mean as much to golf as Bobby Charlton
does to swimming, but we have a hell of a time. It does the
heart good being around the old faces, taking the mickey, and
enjoying the company of the men who did it the hard way.

There have been softer earners. I've appeared in several TV
commercials, films, and did two stage plays. The first with the
late Jack Magowan, *Shadow of a Gunman,* a story of the Irish
uprising, was at the Mermaid Theatre. I'm told everyone in
the back row could hear me thundering around as the brutish
British sergeant. I was only acting. The other, *Inside Out,* was
at the Royal Court (a right posh thespian I was becoming) but
since I couldn't really understand the language of the Nick
(no, I've never flirted with the Law), I knew it wouldn't last
long. It didn't. But since I was not prepared to work a long
run—I'd get too fidgety—it was just as well.

I've taken a few bows, pressed a lot of flesh, and generally
had a good time. Since I lived like a priest during the long
fighting days I made up for it with a drink or two in the mel-

lowing years. But the binges don't last long. I go on the wagon with a boring frequency. If not the faithful Barbara gives me a right nagging.

We've brought up three sons, Terry, Paul and Richard, and daughter Wendy. I'm a proud Grandad of two boys, James and Charlie. The lights of my life. Spoiled rotten. At least the boys had a better chance than me, though we had all the love wanted where I was brought up. They went to Haberdashers' public school. Imagine a Downes captain of the cricket team who went to Sri Lanka and scored the first win for years!

I daren't tell 'em to their faces but I'm proud of the family. They'd think the old man had gone soppy. Never caused Barbara and me the slightest trouble. I've lived the life I wanted, been blessed with a good family, done all the things I ever dreamed of, from birds to booze. I haven't got a lot of money but I haven't got to go out and get any. I'm too old to alter. Accept me as I am.